HE GIVES
and
HE TAKES AWAY

Embracing the sovereignty of God
when grieving the death of a child

the STORY of HANNAH DUFRIN'S
LIFE and DEATH as TOLD by HER MOTHER

Sandy Dufrin

authorHOUSE

1663 LIBERTY DRIVE, SUITE 200
BLOOMINGTON, INDIANA 47403
(800) 839-8640
www.authorhouse.com

First published by AuthorHouse 12/13/05

ISBN: 1-4208-9223-1 (sc)
ISBN: 1-4208-9224-X (dj)

Library of Congress Control Number: 2005910986

Printed in the United States of America
Bloomington, Indiana

This book is printed on acid-free paper.

To Phil

There is no other person I
would choose to share in the
privilege of suffering for Christ.
Thank you for your faithfulness
to me, our family, and most of all,
to Jesus Christ, our Lord and Savior.

In Memory of
Hannah Marie Dufrin
August 2, 1999 – February 8, 2004

She was a delicate flower picked
by God to grace the fields of heaven.

There is time for everything,
and a season for every activity under heaven:
a time to be born and a time to die,
a time to plant and a time to uproot,
a time to kill and a time to heal,
a time to tear down and a time to build,
a time to weep and a time to laugh,
a time to mourn and a time to dance . . . .

ECCLESIASTES 3:1-4
(NIV)

Contents

Acknowledgments 9

Introduction 13

1   *Not As I Will* 19

2   *A Time to be Born* 35

3   *No Regrets* 49

4   *A Time to Die* 71

5   *A Time to Weep* 99

6   *Wedding Plans* 131

7   *A Time to Mourn* 149

8   *A Time to Heal* 165

Epilogue 205

Appendix A:

    A Word About the Sovereignty of God in Suffering 211

Appendix B:

    Help for Parents Whose Child Has Died 217

Appendix C:

    Childlike Faith 229

Appendix D:

    Resources for Grieving Parents 237

Notes 239

ACKNOWLEDGMENTS

To my husband, Phil: Dedicating this book to you is not enough to express my deep appreciation for your enthusiastic praise and assistance. Your affirmation of my abilities, care for the children, and support through the late nights ("I'll get up with the kids"), gave me the encouragement to keep going when I couldn't see the end in sight.

To my friends and sisters in Christ: Helen, Kristi, Janine, Wendy, and Carmen. This book would not have been possible if it weren't for the countless hours of babysitting you provided for my children in one way or another. But even more than this, I am indebted to you for the encouragement and support you showed to me in the year following Hannah's death. You helped me to sort out many of the feelings that are expressed on these pages and have prayed for the grace needed to deal with my emotions. I know that you miss her almost as much as I do. From one mother's heart to another, thank you.

Thank you to the people of Covenant Life Community Church. The support and prayers we received were not only a blessing to our family, but were an example of what it means to show the world we are Christians by our love.

To our family, specifically my parents, Phil's parents, and our many relatives: Without a doubt, we have grieved Hannah's death in a grace-filled manner because of your continual prayers. Thank you for lifting us up before the Lord.

To our children: Moriah, Nathan, Abigail, Samuel, and Aaron. May this book be a testimony of God's faithfulness during the difficult times of life. Hannah's story has become your legacy, and someday I hope that you will pass it down to your children's children, long after I am gone. I am thankful that God has used your sister's death to show you the way to everlasting life through Christ. Keep loving Jesus, and one day, we will all be together again.

To Moriah: A special thank you for the many days when you took over as "Mama" so that I could finish this book. You are a dear, thoughtful daughter who has been gifted with an incredible ability to manage our home!

To Nathan: You have also been a tremendous help to me in so many ways. Most of all, I thank you for taking the initiative to serve me java drinks so that I could make it through the long hours of writing.

To Josh Nunez: Thank you for taking the time to read and edit my manuscript, provide valuable insight, and respond to my endless questions. Because of your giftedness with the written word, I value your opinion greatly. Thank you for giving it to me honestly.

And last but not least, thank you Jesus Christ, my Lord and Savior. To You I give all the glory for the finished work! Thank you for being faithful to help me through this project from the start to the finish. Ultimately, I have done this for You; I pray that You are pleased with me.

In this you greatly rejoice, though now for a little while you may have had to suffer grief in all kinds of trials. These have come so that your faith—of greater worth than gold, which perishes even though refined by fire—may be proved genuine and may result in praise, glory, and honor when Jesus Christ is revealed.

1 PETER 1:6-7
(NIV)

INTRODUCTION
Comfort Overflowing

For just as the sufferings of Christ flow
over into our lives, so also through Christ
our comfort overflows.

2 Corinthians 1:5

I AM THE MOTHER OF AN ORDINARY FAMILY. THERE IS nothing unusual about our lives—we own a home, attend church regularly, and sometimes don't get along too well. Our days are full of routine activity, disciplining children, and creating memories that become the stories we tell over and over. Every family has at least one story to share about their lives, and we are no different. But unlike most ordinary families, our story is about a trial many will never experience in their lifetime: the loss of our beautiful child, Hannah Marie Dufrin.

A week after Hannah's death, I laid in bed one morning, pondering the events of the previous week—her surgery, death, and funeral. I marveled at how faithful God had been to see us through those times and how He supplied joy to ease the pain. My gratitude for God's grace triggered a strong need to testify of His goodness, but I didn't know where to begin. In what way could I encourage others with our experience and help strengthen the faith of those who were facing a difficult time?

A reply came into my mind: *Write her story. You've always wanted to write a book. Write about Hannah.*

Was this God's voice speaking to me? While I don't know for certain, I do believe that He had impressed this desire upon my heart. The story of Hannah's life and death and our journey through grief could be used by God to bring comfort to others, especially to parents who had also lost a child.

Although I was excited about the prospect of writing a book, I still had many reservations concerning the completion of such an overwhelming project. How would I accomplish so big a task, especially with four young children underfoot? Would it be worth the effort? Would our story truly encourage parents who had experienced the pain of a child's death? Would this book help people to recognize God's sovereign hand in all the trials of life? I forced these uncertainties out of my mind, resolving to obey God's call. And that is my primary reason for writing this book—obedience to the will of God. No matter what my hesitation, I knew that He would give me the ability, strength, and confidence to finish the work.

Another reason for sharing our story is the hope that it will help those who are suffering with no end to the pain in sight. Can this testimony speak to the wife whose husband left her with three children for another woman? What about the person who suffers with the excruciating pain of a debilitating illness? Does our situation relate to the parents who just found out that their unborn child has a birth defect?

In each of these scenarios, I believe the answer is yes; our story can help others see through the tears. By looking to Christ alone with our eyes fixed on the hope of eternity, we were able to keep the faith and stay strong by His grace. This same grace is not only reserved for those who have lost a child; it is available to anyone who loves and trusts in Him, no matter what the trial. And to those whom God has spared from suffering, may our story help build your faith during this good season, so that when the trials come, you will stand firm, giving glory and praise to Christ Jesus.

Many of our closest friends have commented, "Losing a child is the worst trial that anyone could experience." There were many times through the process of grief when I would have agreed wholeheartedly with this sentiment. However, we came to realize toward the end of this season, that Hannah's death was difficult but not unbearable. In fact, this trial contained some of the most joyous moments of our lives. This is a shocking statement, I know. But before you close this book and feel you cannot relate, allow me to explain.

The joy that I speak of refers not to my feelings—we are not glad that Hannah is gone. Rather, the inner joy we felt came from seeing the good that resulted from her death: Christ was glorified, the gospel went forth, and we learned to rely on Him for comfort. These were the fruits of our suffering, and the joy we received helped us to endure the pain in our hearts.

It is my earnest hope and prayer that as you read this book you will come away from it saying, "What an awesome God!" and not, "What awesome Christians." God's means of accomplishing His will included the use of prideful, sinful people like ourselves to bring glory to His name. The strength we possessed came *only* from God. The hope we clung to was given *only* through the promises of His Word. The joy we gained grew *only* by the grace and mercy of Him who is faithful. We had little to do with how God accomplished His purpose through Hannah's death. He simply asked us to receive the grace He supplied in answer to the call of suffering.

Come with me now and witness the goodness of God through suffering. I invite you to befriend our family and read how God used the life of a very special four-year-old girl. Walk with us through the pages as I give an account of God's faithfulness during Hannah's birth, illnesses, developmental successes, and surgery. Mourn with us as you read about her death, funeral, and of our lives without her presence. Rejoice with us as you witness how God worked through our suffering to reach others for Christ. Draw comfort for your own trials as you see how God relieved our pain by providing peace and joy.

May this testimony of our ordinary family be an example to you of how simple trust and faith in an extraordinary God *is* possible, even when life doesn't turn out the way we expect. Just as our faith was tested and strengthened through Hannah's life and death, so may yours be also, either in the present trials you face or in the ones that are yet to come.

Author's Note

Unless otherwise noted, the journal entries written before each chapter were taken from a Web page that was created for Hannah in order to com-communicate her progress during surgery and recovery to waiting family and friends.

All Scripture quotations are taken from the New International Version (NIV).

God, by His providence and mercy, is near to us,
orchestrating all the details of this day.
We trust Him.

FEBRUARY 6, 2004
1:30 P.M.

1
Not As I Will

Going a little farther, he fell with his face
to the ground and prayed, "My Father,
if it is possible, may this cup be taken from me.
Yet not as I will, but as you will."

Matthew 26:39

DURING THE BLEAK WINTER MONTHS OF MICHIGAN, IT IS UN-usual to wake up to sunshine streaming through the windows, especially at seven o'clock in the morning. My eyes opened and adjusted to the light which illuminated the unfamiliar surroundings. Where was I? In a second or two I remembered what this day was all about. Today, February 6, 2004, meant heart surgery for our four-year-old daughter, Hannah Marie.

Taking a deep breath, I rolled over and squinted my eyes to look for the source of light. The thick hotel curtains were slightly opened, letting in the morning "hello." My eyes focused on Hannah, who sat on the wide window ledge across the room, wearing her princess nightgown. Phil, my husband of twelve years, stood next to her with his arm wrapped around her waist to keep her from falling. Without them knowing, I listened to their conversation, smiling at the tender interaction between father and daughter.

"Where's the blue truck, Hannah?" asked Phil as he pointed to the construction scene five stories below.

Hannah giggled and tapped the window with her petite finger. "I see it, Daddy!"

"You found it! That's my girl!" cheered Phil as he hugged Hannah a little tighter. Hannah's face beamed with satisfaction. She admired her daddy's opinion and thrived on hearing his praises.

I watched for a minute longer, savoring every second as if in slow motion. I wanted to draw all the pleasure that was possible from this moment, knowing that perhaps one day I might replay it in my mind. I had no idea what God had in store for our family today. We prayed that our desires would be answered affirmatively but also knew that His sovereign purposes would prevail. We trusted His plan no matter what the outcome. Yet I couldn't help but think that this precious time might be one of the last spent with Hannah while here on earth.

Before my mind went too far with the "what ifs" of surgery, I finally spoke and exposed myself as a spy. "Hey, you two! What are you looking at down there?"

Both Hannah and Phil quickly turned to look at me. "Mama!" exclaimed Hannah, as if she was scolding me for secretly watching.

"Sandy, come look at this," Phil said. "It's pretty interesting to watch them work. Hurry! They are about to drive another huge pole into the ground!"

Construction sites never had excited me, especially that early. But Phil and Hannah's enthusiasm was contagious, so I was drawn over to the window. Admittedly, after watching the men work for a while, it was more fascinating than I expected.

"How long have you two been sitting here?" I asked.

"We've been awake for about a half hour. Hannah is really enjoying this!"

Hannah enjoys everything about life, I thought. There aren't too many four-year-old girls who would think a construction site was stimulating morning entertainment.

"Stay there for a minute. I want to get a picture of this." From the opposite side of our hotel room I snapped two pictures of Phil and Hannah as they peered out from behind the curtains to the site below. I wasn't sure if the photos would turn out since the room was still quite dark. It didn't really matter. The scene was etched in my mind even without the help of a photograph.

I tucked the camera back into its case and sat down on the bed, not yet ready to get started with the day. Phil and Hannah continued to share observations about the work below. After a few minutes, Phil turned to me and quietly expressed the summation of his thoughts for the morning: "Let's just take her out of this hospital and go home."

I smiled and gave him a look that agreed with his concern. I didn't have to say anything. Heart surgery was not what we wanted for Hannah, but it was necessary and unavoidable. Phil didn't want this cherished time with Hannah to ever end. In just five hours we would hand her over to the surgical team, entrusting them to mend our daughter's broken heart. Our hearts were broken too, knowing all that Hannah would have to endure. How do we prepare her for this? What words can we use to explain it? Would she ever trust Phil and I again?

I decided to wake myself up by taking a shower. We wanted to be ready early so that the last hours with Hannah would be fully devoted to spending time with her. As the warm water poured over me, I could faintly hear Phil singing to Hannah one of our favorite hymns: "How Great Thou Art." The chorus was the only part she joined in to sing with him.

> Then sings my soul, my Savior God to Thee,
> How great Thou art! How great Thou art!

Hannah had heard this hymn often at home because I frequently played it on the piano. Listening to them bellow out the words was a good reminder of God's faithfulness to me, especially not knowing what the day would hold. God is great and worthy to be praised! I wanted so badly to believe this truth with my whole heart. It would be easy to agree that God is faithful if the surgery went as expected. But what if it didn't? What if Hannah fell into the five percent of those cases where a complication occurred? Would I still be able to say, "How great Thou art?"

Before realizing it I also began singing the hymn while still in the shower. The peace of God came over me, and I smiled while thinking, *Yes, God is faithful and He does understand my fears. I will keep trusting Him with Hannah's life.*

Dressed and my head adorned with a towel, I came out of the bathroom and found Phil and Hannah still sitting on the windowsill. "How about a bath this morning, Hannah?"

"Do you really think she needs one? Didn't you give her one just yesterday morning?" asked Phil.

"Yes, but I want my girl to be squeaky clean for surgery!" Hannah laughed and lifted her arms up to Phil who helped her get down. She loved taking baths, and it wasn't too often that she got to take one alone. Usually she shared the tub with her two-year-old sister, Abigail, and sometimes with her eight-month-old brother, Samuel. This would be considered a treat!

I ran the bath water and helped Hannah to undress. When the water was warm enough I lifted her into the bathtub and helped her to sit down. Hannah's beautiful long brown hair was still in a ponytail; I gently pulled it out and watched it fall to just below her waist. Throughout Hannah's four years we had cut her hair only one time and that was just in the front. The length was never touched, and we couldn't bear the thought of trimming those luscious locks! We often told Hannah that her hair was her "glory" and she was proud to show it off: "Look, Mama!" she would say. "God gave me such beautiful hair."

"Daddy," I called out to Phil, "can you help Hannah in the tub while I finish getting ready?"

"Sure. Do you want me to go fetch you some breakfast from the lobby first? It might be a good idea to eat now since Hannah is occupied and can't see you."

Because of the surgery, Hannah had not been allowed to eat since late the night before. Her last drink of water was at eight o'clock that morning. I was hungry but felt that if Hannah had to go without food, I should, too. On the other hand, if I didn't eat, who knew when I'd get a chance again. This was going to be a long day, and I needed the physical strength to get through the emotional roller coaster of surgery.

I consented to eating a muffin and drinking orange juice while Phil kept Hannah busy in the bathtub. The chorus of "How Great Thou Art" was heard again above the splashing water, as sung by both Phil and Hannah. I quietly joined in with their singing while putting on my makeup just outside the bathroom door.

The blow dryer went on, and I could hear Phil telling Hannah how beautiful her hair was. "Daddy!" squealed Hannah, who always tried to pretend she didn't appreciate compliments.

"Go show Mama your hair," encouraged Phil.

"Look, Mama! Look at my hair!" Hannah flipped her hair from underneath and turned around so that I could see all of it.

"Wow, Hannah! You look beautiful as always. But you don't have any clothes on! Let's get you dressed, OK?"

While packing her suitcase at home, I thought for a while about what would be appropriate for Hannah to wear on the day of her heart surgery. Even though this was going to be a difficult day for all of us, it was a very special day too, one that deserved extra attention. I wanted Hannah to feel proud—this was her moment! God was going to heal her heart, using the hands of a world-renowned surgeon, Dr. Bove (pronounced bo-VAY). Every night while tucking Hannah into bed, we prayed that God would heal her heart, if it be His will. Up to this point, the Lord had not chosen to give Hannah a new heart supernaturally. He did, however, make a way for her defective heart to be repaired, good as new. We felt blessed that God was answering our prayers, even if it wasn't in the way we expected.

I pulled a pink and white long-sleeve shirt over Hannah's head. "Look, Hannah. Mama picked out the shirt with hearts on it for today because this afternoon, you're going to have heart surgery."

Hannah seemed to like my choice in clothing, but she didn't respond at all to my comment about heart surgery. Phil and I tried many times to explain the surgery in a way that she could understand. We were honest with Hannah about the experience, telling her that the doctors were going to fix her heart and it would hurt. We assured her that during the surgery she would be asleep and not feel a thing. When the surgery was over, Mama and Daddy would be right there to see her when she woke up.

"I don't like that!" was Hannah's only negative comment. She never cried or protested. If Mama and Daddy said that this was good for Hannah, then she trusted our judgment. Oh, how I prayed that we were making the right decision!

"Let me fix your hair." This was Hannah's signal to snuggle between my knees and turn around so that we could face the full-length mirror. The policy for surgery stated that all hair must be pulled up into a ponytail. This is how we usually managed Hannah's long hair anyway.

"Sit still, Hannah!" I exclaimed. She never was very good at holding steady so that I could make it smooth on top. Hannah was having too much fun watching her silly antics in the mirror to bother with keeping still. I was getting frustrated, but this wasn't unusual either—it always took two or three attempts to make her hair just right.

After putting in the ponytail I tied a satin pink ribbon into a bow around the band. Hair ribbons are not worn much by little girls these days, but I think they are adorable. Hannah's hair accessory box at home was full of them, of all different types, sizes, and colors.

Now that Hannah's hair was done, it was time to focus on my own. With curling iron in hand I made the finishing touches. Phil and Hannah waited patiently by playing a game about ice cream called Scoops. Ever since Christmas, Scoops had been her favorite game, and she asked to play it several times each day. At first, Phil and I enjoyed the game because it brought Hannah so much joy, but it wasn't long before we grew weary of Hannah's relentless nagging! After playing one round it was back to the window to check on the progress of the construction site below.

The time was nearing 10 a.m., and we wanted to get started on our walk around the hospital. We thought Hannah would enjoy getting out of the hotel room where she could burn some pent-up energy. I quickly finished tidying up our room and gathered together the bags we needed to take for the day. Before leaving the room I grabbed the camera and called Hannah and Phil over from the window. "Let me take a picture of you, Hannah. You look so pretty!"

Hannah had never been very photogenic. (I'm her mother so I can say that honestly.) She had a hard time looking straight ahead at the camera even though I tried everything to get her attention, short of doing back flips!

In spite of this, while Hannah wasn't always looking at the camera directly, her smile never failed. There was rarely a moment when Hannah wasn't smiling, no matter if the camera was pointed her way or not. She had such a joyful and peaceful spirit about her, one that drew attention every place we went. Hannah's smile was contagious, and all who noticed her couldn't help but smile in return.

"Your turn, Sandy. There are never enough pictures of you with the kids. Hop in next to Hannah."

I squatted down to Hannah's level and draped my left arm around her backside. Phil snapped the picture, and then we traded spots. Hannah wrapped her arms around Phil, and they held each other close. I zoomed in on their faces and exclaimed, "Wow! What a great picture this will be!" The thought briefly entered my mind that this might possibly be Hannah's last photograph. But just as soon as the thought came, I quickly put it out of my mind. *That's not going to happen to us! Hannah is going to be just fine.* This was one of the few times I considered the possibility of Hannah dying during heart surgery. Certainly the surgery was risky, but we were assured that the chance of death was minimal.

The three of us went hand-in-hand out the door with a backpack full of things to keep Hannah busy while waiting. I also carried a bag of books and my knitting project, both meant to keep my mind occupied while Hannah was in surgery. Because our hotel room was conveniently connected to the hospital, we didn't have to carry our coats. If there was anything we needed or forgot to bring, our room was less than five minutes from the surgical waiting area.

We decided to head down to the first floor and find the gift shop. Hannah pushed the elevator buttons herself, a privilege she rarely enjoyed since her eight-year-old sister, Moriah, and six-year-old brother, Nathan, were quicker and never gave her the opportunity.

"Look, Mama! One!" exclaimed Hannah as we stepped off the elevator. Hannah had just begun to learn her letters and numbers in our homeschool. I was surprised that she could recognize the oversized number "1" on the wall opposite the elevator.

"Great job, Hannah! You found the number one! Hooray!" We genuinely celebrated every small milestone of Hannah's life. For the first two years she struggled to stay healthy and was developmentally delayed in several areas. But recently, Hannah showed promise in catching up to her peers. Our other children learned their numbers and letters easily at a young age. It took a long time for Hannah to come this far, and we were sincerely overjoyed and proud of her progress.

We were in and out of the gift shop in just a few minutes. Hannah wanted to stay and play with the toys for sale, so we quickly left before she became captivated.

Our hospital tour continued as we strolled through the halls, maneuvering ourselves around the crowds. Several times as we passed people walking by, we noticed their eyes being drawn to Hannah. Smiling they would say, "Hello" or comment, "How cute!" Hannah loved every minute of it! She always had a way of drawing attention, especially with her big dark brown eyes and, of course, that infectious smile! It was not unusual for Hannah to attract notice from complete strangers, even when the other four children were with us. Hannah stood out without having to say a word. There was a peacefulness about her that was enchanting. She was often the focal point, not only that day, but everywhere we went as a family.

Just before 11 a.m. we started heading toward the pediatric surgical waiting room on the third floor. The University of Michigan Hospital complex was enormous, but thankfully there were signs posted everywhere, directing us to Mott Children's Hospital.

Taking those steps towards the hospital unexpectedly changed something in our countenance. There was a seriousness about the situation that wasn't there before. We were embarking on the long hard road of heart surgery, and our lives were about to become intense. Our emotions changed from delight over Hannah to the soberness one feels when facing a trial head on. It was surreal.

Phil and I refused to let Hannah sense our true feelings. We wanted her to enjoy our last moments before surgery without fear or worry. "Ready, Hannah? One . . . two . . . three!" Holding Hannah's hands on both sides, we lifted her up by the arms high into the air. Her legs flew up, and then her feet fell back down to the floor with a thud. "Again!" she would squeal, and we always gave in.

The temptation to give Hannah anything she asked for was so great; thank goodness she didn't realize it! Although her medical condition required us to care more for her physical needs, our behavioral expectations were not different than those of our other children. She was not the "favorite child" or loved more because of all she had endured through illness. Hannah's sisters and brothers knew that she was created special by God, but this did not inhibit them from treating her the same, both in times of peace and conflict!

The surgical registration desk was not foreign to us. Back in October of 2002, Hannah had her tonsils and adenoids removed at Mott Hospital. Several of the nurses and staff who assisted us during that time were familiar, and some recognized Hannah as well. We checked in ten minutes early and filled out the necessary forms. It appeared that Hannah's surgery was still scheduled for noon; there had been a fear of it being postponed due to an emergency surgery. It was so much effort getting to this point. I would not have been able to handle the disappointment of having to reschedule!

A concern over rescheduling Hannah's surgery wasn't the only thing we were anxious about. While we didn't often struggle over the life or death implications of surgery, Phil and I wondered most about the pain that Hannah would undergo and our ability to comfort her. Would our four-year-old daughter feel betrayed that we had let the surgeons hurt her? What if the doctors were wrong about her recovery? They had assured us that all measures would be taken to guarantee that Hannah was not in pain. If all went according to plan, two weeks after the surgery she would be running around again as if nothing happened.

Yet there was no denying the possible complications. Hannah's recovery might be slower than expected and more agonizing. She could require a pacemaker or need additional surgery in the future should the heart muscle grow back. Those were the fears that Phil and I grappled with in the days leading to surgery. We continually prayed for a good result but always added, "Your will be done" to those prayers. Unmistakably, God's grace was strongly upon us as we did not focus on the possibility of Hannah's death, thus tainting our last joyful moments together before surgery.

The small waiting room was full that day, but we found two seats that allowed us to be somewhat secluded from the stares of others. Sitting directly behind us was a young lady who volunteered at the hospital regularly, using her God-given talent to bless others with the peaceful music of the harp. The music was soothing to our souls and allowed us to calm down and relax during the wait.

At first we kept Hannah seated on our laps, holding her closely. She didn't mind snuggling with her daddy or mama, especially while clutching "Blankie" and sucking her thumb. At one point a nurse walked by and asked, "Would you like me to get some toys for Hannah to play with?" Although the room had plenty of toys, she must have thought that Hannah was sitting on our laps because there wasn't anything else to do.

"No, thank you," I answered. "Selfishly we want her to sit on our laps for as long as possible." The nurse smiled and nodded as if she understood the emotions we were having about the surgery.

"Hannah?" called out another nurse. I took Hannah's hand and led her into an examination room within the waiting area. The nurse asked me several questions, took Hannah's temperature, and gave her a hospital gown to wear. Children who spend the majority of their lives in hospitals or at the doctor's office tend to be more apprehensive when placed in medical situations. Not so for our brave girl! As long as I remained with her, Hannah was quite tolerant of most medical procedures.

But on that day for some reason, her outside appearance became the priority over displaying a courageous spirit. Hannah actually became distraught about having to wear the hospital gown! Through teary eyes my normally compliant child had no trouble telling me that she did not want to take her clothes off. I gently reassured Hannah that all of the other children having surgery would also be wearing a gown. It didn't seem to matter.

I carried Hannah out of the exam room as she shed big tears. Phil and I exchanged smirks. Seeing Hannah upset over her clothing was humorous, especially knowing that there were bigger things to be stressed about. Now was a good time to show Hannah the toys and books we had brought with us. The distraction helped her to stop crying quickly.

Another stipulation for surgery was that articles of clothing containing metal could not be worn, including jewelry or barrettes. Because Hannah's hair band had a small section of metal, we had to pull it out, leaving her hair long and flowing. I knew that Hannah's hair could not be left this way, as it would be difficult for the surgical nurses to manage, and Hannah would certainly not be comfortable.

I asked a nurse if she might have a different hair band, one without metal. Around the corner into another room she went, returning in less than a minute with a whole assortment of bands.

"Which color would you like, Hannah?" the nurse asked.

It didn't take Hannah long to make up her mind. "Pink," she answered shyly. Using the comb from my purse I pulled up Hannah's hair and tied it again with the pink ribbon. Ashamedly, I was proud of Hannah's hair, perhaps too proud. One would think that the seriousness of surgery would cause me to be less concerned over how Hannah's hair looked. How often I needlessly fussed over making it look just right!

The clock was ticking closer to 12 p.m. The waiting room began to empty out as other children were called for surgery. Hannah kept busy playing with her Leap Pad, coloring pictures, and reading books. She didn't stay attentive to one task for too long. We also found this to be true when at home. Usually Hannah's short attention span was somewhat exasperating for me, a busy mother of five. But today, with all my love and devotion focused on one little girl, I didn't mind.

Together the three of us laughed and played as the minutes passed. Phil and I were nervous, but we didn't want Hannah to suspect it. Every time a doctor walked into the waiting room, both of us would look up and hold our breath. Was it our turn? No, not yet—a few more minutes of precious time to be spent with Hannah. Each additional moment was seen as a gift from God who allowed us to make more joyful memories with our daughter.

Our surgery time came and went. By now the waiting room was completely empty. Hannah wanted to watch television at the back of the room, and we conceded. Phil was getting more anxious, thinking that the morning surgery went longer than expected, thereby postponing our surgery altogether. He inquired at the receptionist's desk, and we were assured that Hannah's surgery was still on schedule. Things were just running behind, which from our previous hospital experience we knew was quite typical.

Shortly before 1 p.m., a nurse came into the waiting room and stood at the desk for a great length of time, chatting with the other staff. Phil and I both noticed that she had come in, but didn't think too much of it. We went on begrudgingly watching *Barney* as Hannah sat engrossed. Finally the nurse hollered, "Hannah?"

My heart jumped! Was it time?

"Yes," Phil answered. "This is Hannah Dufrin."

"Oh!" she exclaimed. "At first we didn't see you sitting down there." I thought, *How could you not? We're the only people here!*

"It's time to go then!" she yelled out. Most of the medical personnel at U of M were pleasant and gentle. This nurse, although kind, was somewhat rough. Didn't she know what we were facing? Why didn't she have more compassion? I didn't say any of these words out loud, but my mind screamed them. Later Phil told me that he was also highly irritated. Perhaps God used this woman to help us relieve some of the intense emotions we were feeling. Instead of being anxious or worried, we were annoyed!

Following the nurse, Phil carried Hannah down the long hall to the surgical holding room. The nurse rattled on about this or that, and I politely countered, "Oh, really. I see. Interesting," none of which I seriously meant. Hannah was oblivious to our destination. She enjoyed being held tightly in her daddy's arms and appreciated the new scenery.

The surgical holding room hadn't changed from our previous visit. Even the nurse-in-charge was the same person. I sat down in a comfortable wooden rocking chair and placed Hannah on my lap.

The nurse explained that a few members of Dr. Bove's surgical team would soon come out to speak with us. She also said that shortly before surgery, Hannah would be given a drug called Versed. It would help her to relax, and, although still physically conscious, she wouldn't remember us leaving her. I was relieved. This was the part of surgery that I dreaded most of all—handing Hannah over to the doctors and nurses. Certainly she would cry. Would she scream, "Mama! No!" and hold out her arms for me?

This was not the way I wanted to remember our last moments together before surgery. More than any other aspect of surgery, I often prayed that our parting would not be fraught with tears, both hers and ours. The Versed was a direct answer to those prayers. If only they could have prescribed some of that drug for us, too!

The anesthesiologist and two of Dr. Bove's nurses came in to answer any last-minute questions. We were reassured that Dr. Bove was the best surgeon in the world for this type of surgery. If in the identical situation themselves, Dr. Bove would be the surgeon they would ask for. I don't believe these were just comforting words every parent is told before their child's surgery. The nurses had worked closely with Dr. Bove for almost twenty years. We had no doubt that Hannah was in the best hands.

Phil wanted a moment to sit with Hannah, so I handed her over to him. While on his lap, the nurse gave Hannah the oral dose of Versed, and she took it without objection. After just a few minutes, the drug began to take affect. Hannah looked drowsy but had a big smile on her face. We laughed and teased her for being so happy at a time like this. Surprisingly, I felt happy, too! Even though our precious daughter was about to undergo invasive heart surgery, this moment was not clouded with fear or anxiety—quite the opposite from what we expected. God was giving us an unexplainable peace.

It was officially time for us to say good-bye to Hannah. Phil embraced our daughter's limp body and kissed her all over. He told her one last time, "Daddy and Mama won't be with you, but Jesus will. He will never leave you. I love you, Hannah." I held her briefly on my lap again, hugging her close and whispering, "I'll see you soon. Mama loves you, Sweet Girl."

I was drawn to place my hand gently over Hannah's chest. I felt her heart beating and closed my eyes. In just under an hour her heart would not pump on its own, and a machine would take over as the surgeons worked. In just two hours her heart would be healed by the surgeon's hand. In just three hours her heart would beat stronger, no longer broken. And in just four hours I would feel her heart beating again . . . . *Lord, please let her live.*

The nurse brought in a little red wagon lined with soft pillows. Phil took Hannah from my arms and placed her gently into the wagon. Instead of crying out for us, Hannah smiled innocently with a look of acceptance and trust. We couldn't help but smile in return; our eyes were dry. I had anticipated a heart-wrenching separation as the nurses pulled a screaming Hannah from my arms. The Lord's grace was covering the three of us as we parted.

We watched from behind the wagon as Hannah was wheeled away to the operating room. "Good-bye, Hannah! We love you!"

She turned slightly and looked over her shoulder for one last glance at her daddy and mama. A little hand rose up and weakly waved good-bye. The nurse said, "Don't worry. We'll take good care of her."

Yes, we were confident that Hannah would be well cared for. But we also knew that it was the Lord who would be caring for Hannah overall. From the day of her birth, through all her illnesses, and in the last weeks leading to this moment, Phil and I had repeatedly given our daughter back to Him. Now, facing heart surgery, we surrendered our will to God once more and continued to trust Him with Hannah's life.

Please Lord, bring her back to my aching arms. Let me hold my little girl again.

Thy will be done.

*We gave Hannah over to God a long time ago, and
we have learned from all her medical ups-and-downs that
He is in complete control. God has made Hannah
this way, and He has a plan for her life. Whatever the
outcome, I know that we will continue to trust in His
plan for our lives.*

JANUARY 30, 2004
10:45 P.M.

2
A Time to Be Born

For you have been my hope, O Sovereign LORD,
my confidence since my youth.
From birth I have relied on you;
you brought me forth from my mother's womb.
I will ever praise you.

"Hannah's Psalm"
Psalm 71:5-6

"A GIRL! WE HAVE ANOTHER DAUGHTER!" PHIL WHISPERED in my ear.

The date was August 2, 1999. Our third child, Hannah Marie Dufrin, made her entrance into the world shortly before midnight. I had been in labor since noon and was tired but relieved that the questions surrounding Hannah's health could now be answered. At first she had difficulty breathing, but Hannah perked up and appeared healthy, strong, and normal, something we hadn't been sure about from the sixth month of pregnancy until now.

The trouble began at the twenty-fifth week of pregnancy when I was measuring seven weeks further along. We thought about the possibility of twins and would have welcomed this double blessing joyously. However, our hopes were quickly dashed when an ultrasound revealed that I was carrying double the amount of amniotic fluid, and the baby had a large head. The perinatologist suspected that our baby might have Down's Syndrome, so he suggested that we have an amniocentesis to verify this diagnosis.

Waiting for the test results was one of the most trying times of my life. I wanted to trust God's plan, but at the same time was very grieved over the loss of a "normal" child. Was this the reason we had experienced hesitation about having another child in the first place? Was God trying to keep us from going through this sorrow and we did not heed Him?

Before Hannah was conceived, we sincerely sought the Lord's guidance as to whether or not we should have a third child. The year was 1998, and there was much doomsday talk surrounding a possible world disaster due to Y2K. Would it be wise to bring another mouth to feed into this world? We wanted to have another child, but even more we wanted to do God's will. I was saddened with the thought that God might not want us to have any more children, but I was also willing to accept it.

Phil and I prayed both separately and together, seeking the Lord's will and guidance from the Word. We found no Scriptures opposing the conception of children, during good times or bad. After a time, we received peace about this decision, reasoning that God certainly would not discourage more children to be raised for His glory.

In early December of 1998 I became pregnant, and we rejoiced over our new blessing. I wrote in my journal, "I believe that the enemy tried to prevent us from enlarging our family because he knows the defeat of adding another warrior to the kingdom of God." Now I wondered if all the doubt and resistance we felt meant that our third child would grow to do great things for the Lord.

With the possibility of having a Down's Syndrome child before us, I had trouble envisioning our child inspiring others to great faith. We had prayed for God to guide our decision to have another child, and now were doubting if we heard His answer correctly. Obviously, with thoughts like these, we were not firmly grounded in the truth that God is sovereign. We always believed that God was in control, but our faith had not yet been tested in this area.

We asked for prayer from our church family and faithfully received this along with so much more. Never before had I been so covered in prayer. Not only were our family and friends praying, but so were other believers—people we had never met. I heard many stories of those who were touched by the Lord as a result of praying for our baby, and how the Spirit moved phenomenally while interceding for us. This third child, for whom we had many doubts about conceiving, was already being used by God for His purposes.

After five days of waiting, the amniocentesis results for Down's Syndrome came back negative. For now this test was over, and we had kept our faith and trust in God. Throughout the remaining fourteen weeks of pregnancy I felt much peace and enjoyed the growth and movement of our baby within me.

From the day she was born, Hannah was a content, easygoing baby. All those prayers must have had an effect not only on her health, but also on her disposition! The size of Hannah's head caused the doctors to be concerned, but they couldn't find anything wrong with her. She nursed well, slept through the night by six weeks, and was developmentally on track. We praised God for His faithfulness in her life. Yet just when we thought that Hannah was in the clear, the Lord wanted to test our faithfulness to Him once more.

At four months of age, our lives took a different turn. Hannah woke up with a cold one morning. She coughed a little throughout the day and was congested, but I didn't think much of it. The following day her cold seemed a little worse, and as the day progressed it was obvious that Hannah was in serious trouble.

I called our doctor who told us to bring her to the After-Hours Clinic at Sparrow Hospital in Lansing. The doctors examined Hannah and saw that she was having a difficult time breathing. Her chest was retracting, a sign that she was working hard to take a breath. Because of Hannah's age, they decided to admit her to the hospital for observation and treatment.

Once admitted, Hannah's ability to breathe did not improve even with frequent breathing treatments. She labored so hard to inhale that the doctors were concerned she wouldn't have any energy left to continue breathing. So they transferred Hannah over to the Intensive Care Unit where medical staff could monitor her more closely. Doctors did what they could to help her breathe, but nothing worked. The only remaining option was to hook Hannah up to a ventilator that would do the breathing for her.

A tube was placed down Hannah's throat and into her lungs. A large machine with many dials and digital displays sat next to her crib. When Phil and I were allowed to see Hannah after the procedure, we could hardly recognize her. Seven different tubes came in and out of her body. She was on paralyzing medication and sedatives and couldn't respond at all to our touch or voice.

The first few days were the most difficult to cope with. Tests confirmed that Hannah had Respiratory Syncytial Virus (RSV), a virus that in most people presents itself as the common cold but can be life-threatening for a small infant. Chest X-rays showed that her lungs were filled with pneumonia. The ventilator was set quite high, giving Hannah maximum support to breathe. Phil and I never left her side as we quietly watched the medical team decide on the best treatment for Hannah. At times we weren't sure if she would pull through.

Wavering between life and death was the hardest part of this ordeal. All we could do was pray and trust God for the life of our baby girl. Hundreds of people were praying for Hannah, and this helped us to remain calm and not fall apart. Yes, there were moments when we were scared and distraught over the state of her health, but we continued to give Hannah back to the Lord, knowing that He was holding her in His hands.

While hospitalized, the doctors also found that Hannah's heart was not normal. Tests showed Hannah was in the early stage of Hypertrophic Cardiomyopathy, a congenital defect which causes the heart muscle of the left ventricle to grow thicker over time. The doctors suspected that this abnormality was taking energy away from Hannah's body and not allowing her to effectively fight off illness. This could explain why the RSV had been so hard on Hannah compared to other children in whom the virus presents itself as a common cold.

The doctors also discovered Hannah had low muscle tone, causing the movements of her arms and legs to be floppy. Together with Hannah's large head and the cardiomyopathy, doctors began to suspect a genetic disorder. A handful of tests for obvious disorders, such as Cystic Fibrosis, were administered, all with negative results. The doctors were puzzled. A specific diagnosis might present itself more clearly as Hannah grew, but for now, the main goal was to restore her health after the bout with RSV.

After eleven days, doctors were able to remove the ventilator, and Hannah succeeded at breathing on her own. As the new year turned, we held our breath and waited from the hospital room to see if all the predictions about Y2K would come to pass. On January 1, our fears were relieved, and we laughed at ourselves for being so indecisive about conceiving another child. We had no regrets about bringing a third child into the world, even though Hannah's health was uncertain, and the pain of watching her struggle to recover was difficult to bear.

Phil and I never imagined that Hannah would be hospitalized for such a great length of time. After twenty-three days had passed, she was well enough to go home but still fragile. Doctor appointments, in-home nursing care, and visits with physical and occupational therapists became part of our everyday life. We began to meet with several specialists who attempted to find a name for Hannah's unknown syndrome. None was found. In our minds, we didn't need a name for her condition—it truly did not matter. We had learned to trust God for Hannah's future, and although difficult to talk about, we were willing to accept His plan even if it meant she would go home to be with Him.

During the next eighteen months, Hannah was admitted to the hospital a total of nine times, mostly due to respiratory distress from cold viruses. The RSV had damaged Hannah's lungs so severely that every cold she contracted resulted in a three to seven day stay at the hospital. Hannah's heart condition also complicated her health, making her more susceptible to illness.

We spent the majority of the winter isolated at home to protect her from germs. Moriah and Nathan were not allowed to play with other children for fear of passing sickness on to Hannah. Being home was definitely challenging, but we made the best of it and tried to include little Hannah in our creative fun. One time the children and I declared it "Pioneer Day," and we dressed up as the characters from *Little House on the Prairie:* I, of course, was Ma, Moriah was Laura, Nathan was Albert, and Hannah was Baby Carrie!

In June of 2000, when Hannah was not even a year old, she became critically ill again with pneumonia. Upon seeing Hannah's small, frail body, the doctors decided that it was time to fatten her up. A gastronomy tube was surgically placed in her stomach, and at the same time, surgeons removed a small piece of muscle from her upper thigh for a biopsy. Hannah's large medical team hoped they would finally have an answer as to why she was constantly sick and not thriving. The feeding tube proved to be a success and helped provide Hannah with additional calories, but the result of the biopsy concluded absolutely nothing. Doctors were stumped. Hannah's condition remained a mystery.

After twenty-six days, Hannah had improved enough to be brought home and cared for by her family. Doctors only agreed to discharge her if we also took home a feeding machine, bi-pap breathing machine, oxygen, and pulse oximeter. On top of this demanding health regimen, the cardiomyopathy had worsened to the point where medication was also needed three times a day. Her bedroom looked more like a hospital room than a nursery.

Phil and I were so glad to bring Hannah home that we didn't care what was required of us. The sleepless nights, continuous medical appointments, medications, and therapy were worth enduring for the sake of being a family again. Many people commented, "I don't know how you are able to take care of Hannah's needs without falling apart!"

"You would do it too if she were your daughter," we'd reply. "We've learned to rely on God's strength and not on our own."

Hannah's second year of life showed more promise than the first. She still required the machines and isolation to keep from getting sick, but we were pleased to see her gaining weight and developing. At twelve months of age, Hannah learned to sit up without support. At eighteen months she developed her own unusual method of locomotion. By scooting around the floor on her bottom, Hannah's world opened up as she explored the house and began to engage in mischievous activity.

I remember the time when Hannah scooted into the bathroom and discovered a box of Moriah's plastic play food. (Don't ask me why it was in there to begin with!) Coming upon the scene later I discovered that Hannah had dropped several of the toys into the toilet! Normally I would have been frustrated with this naughty behavior, but instead I was so glad that she had done something a normal toddler would do!

A few months following her second birthday, we celebrated the long-awaited day when Hannah would walk on her own. Specially-made orthopedic foot braces kept her feet from rolling in as she clomped unsteadily across the kitchen floor. When the summer ended and therapy started up again, we couldn't wait to show the therapists Hannah's new developmental success. The progress she had made throughout that year was the collective result of a lot of hard work and patience from many caregivers and professionals. Each milestone was seen as a blessing by everyone who knew her.

Another blessing worth mentioning was the conception of a fourth child. God surprised us with this pregnancy, and we wondered how to manage it all. Yet knowing that Hannah would have a new brother or sister to play with caused us to rejoice.

One month before the baby was due, we decided it was time to take Hannah off her nighttime gastronomy tube feedings. We thought that she was consuming enough calories throughout the day to sustain her. Our speculation proved to be right, and the doctors agreed to remove the tube. Having already been taken off the breathing machine and pulse oximeter months earlier, Hannah was free from any machines. Just in time too, as the demands of a newborn baby became our focus. A new sister, Abigail Ann, arrived in late May of 2001 when Hannah was just twenty-two months old.

When Phil brought our children to the hospital to meet Abigail for the first time, Hannah's reaction surprised me. I had thought that at so young an age she would not really understand what it meant to have a new sister. But when Phil plopped Hannah on my bed and pointed to the bassinet where Baby lay sleeping, she took one look, grinned from ear to ear, and giggled hysterically! We couldn't help but join with her in the laughter! Hannah's amusement over the newest Dufrin was a sign that she and Abigail were already on their way to becoming the best of friends.

Between the ages of two and three, Hannah began to speak. A speech therapist was added to the list of therapists we saw in our home on a regular basis. When Hannah became proficient with the spoken word, there was no stopping her. She talked incessantly, and this eventually led to a habit of relentless nagging:

"Mama, play a game?"

"I can't right now, Hannah. I'm making dinner."

"Mama, color with me?"

"I'm busy making dinner, Hannah. Maybe later."

"Mama, read story?"

"Hannah! I've already told you that I can't. Please, go into the living room and let me cook, OK?"

"Mama, play a game?"

And on and on it went!

Hannah reached each developmental goal set by her therapists and was making phenomenal progress. Because her health issues seemed to be under control, Hannah's body could now concentrate more intently on developing in other ways. From what we could observe and from what psychological tests showed, Hannah was not retarded in any way. The frequent illnesses she suffered throughout the first two years of life caused her cognitive capabilities to be delayed. Eventually Hannah would do all the things a normal child could do, just at a slower pace.

The quest to find a name for Hannah's syndrome continued to baffle the specialists she saw on a regular basis. No one had answers. There was no history of any similar disorder in either my family or Phil's. The tests for Dwarfism and Noonan's Syndrome both came back negative. Doctors may have been frustrated by their inability to diagnosis Hannah, but we didn't care one bit. God had made her this way to suit His purpose, and this was all we needed to know.

Those who knew Hannah rarely thought of her as different. Phil and I treated her the same as our other children. We did not excuse improper behavior because she "had been through so much." Hannah was disciplined, corrected, and trained just like the two who came before her, but with one huge difference: She seldom needed it!

The only defiance that Hannah showed was when we purposively asked her to model it: "Hannah, give me some attitude." This was her signal to cross her arms, thrust out a hip, and scowl. This pose never quite fit Hannah; she couldn't convincingly demonstrate rebellion even if she tried to fake it! We also frequently ordered Hannah to be insolent: "Give me some hips!" Immediately, she placed her hands on her waist (she had no hips), bent over at the middle, and stuck out her chin as if to say, "I'm in charge here. You can't make me do anything!" We'd all get a good laugh, Hannah included. She always knew that we were just joking, and she never learned true defiance from those gestures.

Like all children, Hannah was a sinner from birth, but there was something sweet about her countenance that caused her to be more compliant. During those rare times when she did require discipline, Hannah's will broke so easily, and she repented with big tears while saying "forgive me" to the one she offended.

Hannah was also a very affectionate child. The pain and suffering she endured did not cause her to distrust people or to pull away from us. Before learning to talk, Hannah demonstrated her love by using a hand signal that Phil had taught her. "Hannah, do you love me?" he would ask. She always replied by giving a "thumbs up" and placing her fist over her heart. "Thank you, Hannah," Phil answered back. "I love you, too."

In October of 2003, Hannah had an unexpected victory. Finally at the age of four, she potty trained side-by-side with Abigail—no more diapers! Several months before I had tried potty training Hannah by herself, but she was not ready. In fact, using the toilet became a rather dramatic experience; a flood of tears accompanied each trip to the bathroom.

Nothing had helped Hannah control her bladder, not rewards, threats, bribes, or enthusiastic praise. But on the day when two-year-old Abigail refused to wear diapers, Hannah decided that she would not be outdone by her younger sister. The two offered support to each other through the frequent accidents and gave praise when success was made. This is just one example of the many times when Abigail "pushed" Hannah into doing things that she was not comfortable with. I believe that is one reason why God gave Abigail to us when He did—Hannah needed the encouragement in order to grow.

Also in the fall of that year, we opted to pull Hannah out of physical and occupational therapy, deciding that developing these skills while surrounded by four siblings would bring better results. Hannah's speech was coming along nicely, but she still required a little help once a week with Mrs. Meade, the speech therapist at Williamston Elementary School. Phil and I also made the difficult decision to homeschool Hannah instead of sending her to the special-needs preschool class offered by our school system. It was an experiment to see if she would progress through my tutoring at home, and the results showed that Hannah had blossomed, learning more and more each day. She loved to sit in her seat and do "school," which typically included her favorite activities: coloring, cutting, puzzles, and games. I enjoyed working with Hannah to improve her skills, and she thrived on the individual attention.

In the midst of all this success, Hannah's health problems reared up once again. Hannah's heart muscle in the left ventricle had grown thicker despite the medication's attempts at slowing down the growth. Because of this thickening, the flow of blood out of the aorta was being obstructed, causing the heart to work harder to compensate.

An initial meeting in October of 2003 with the cardiologist at Mott Children's Hospital in Ann Arbor began to prepare us for the inevitable—open heart surgery. We always assumed that heart surgery would be in Hannah's future, but we never expected that it would be so soon. The cardiomyopathy had progressed to a serious level rather quickly, and the doctors wondered if this more aggressive form was somehow related to her unknown syndrome.

There was some debate among the physicians regarding the ideal time to schedule the surgery. In the end, all agreed that it was in Hannah's best interest to go forward as soon as possible. They expected her to recover from the surgery without complication, thus improving her overall health. The heart muscle was not anticipated to grow back again, therefore no additional surgery would be required in the future. However, since every patient responded differently, it was hard to determine what the real need for future surgery might be.

In late January of 2004, we met with Dr. Bove to discuss the particulars of the surgery and to set a date. The surgery itself was called Left Ventricle Myomectomy, which in layman's terms means to cut away the excess heart muscle. Dr. Bove explained that he would not have to make an incision on Hannah's heart but would go into her heart through the aorta instead. If all went well, surgery would take about three hours. He reassured us that there was a ninety-five percent rate of success and only a five percent chance of complication. We had nothing to worry about.

A few people counseled us to obtain a second opinion or to research other facilities that might be more specialized in this type of surgery. But after talking with Dr. Bove and his staff, we needed to look no further than U of M. Mott Children's Hospital is one of the top two hospitals in the country for pediatric cardiac care, and Dr. Bove is one of the top two physicians in the world for pediatric cardiac surgery! Each day, surgeons at Mott perform two or three similar heart surgeries, totaling about 1,000 surgeries per year. We were thankful to God that Ann Arbor is so close to Williamston, and we were fully confident this was the right hospital and the best surgeon to take care of our little girl.

On Friday, February 6, 2004, Dr. Bove had one surgical time open due to a cancellation. If we decided to wait beyond this date, the surgery could not be scheduled for another two months. Phil looked at me and asked, "What do you think? February sixth is only two weeks away. Do you think we can be ready?"

Like Phil, I wanted to set the date as soon as possible and work hard to prepare ourselves rather than anxiously wait another two months. "Yes, let's go ahead with it. We'll be ready."

So it was decided. Although it appeared that we had the choice between the February date or some time in the future, God was the One who ultimately planned this date before the creation of time, according to His sovereign will.

Heart surgery would be the most difficult mountain to cross on Hannah's health journey from birth until age four. Throughout the years, God was with us during all the setbacks and hospitalizations, and we were certain He would help us again. A letter that I wrote to Hannah on her first birthday summarizes this perspective:

> On your first birthday I look at your small, frail body and see a mighty warrior for the Lord inside. You have inspired so many, including Daddy and me. We both can honestly say that we wouldn't trade this past year for anything, even if it meant that God would heal your heart and you never saw another hospital again. Our experiences with you have brought us closer to God as we learn to trust in His sovereignty.

You are indeed a special creation by God with a unique purpose. How excited I am to see what God will do with your life. I hope and pray that your testimony will help you to trust in His plan all of your days.

Heart surgery was another test of our faith to see if we still trusted His plan. Would we pass or fail? Would we continue looking to Christ even if things didn't turn out as we wanted?

At this point, only God knew those answers.

This doesn't seem real. The seriousness of surgery hasn't really hit us yet. There are glimpses every now and then of what will or could happen, but we quickly put them out of our mind and concentrate on Hannah. I believe this is God's grace upon us, and I am thankful for the confidence that He has supplied.

For our light and momentary troubles are achieving for us an eternal glory that far outweighs them all. So we fix our eyes not on what is seen, but what is unseen. For what is seen is temporary, but what is unseen is eternal.
2 Corinthians 4:17-18

We are fixing our eyes on Christ. He can be trusted with Hannah's life, and we look to Him for our comfort.

FEBRUARY 5, 2004
3:26 P.M.

3
No Regrets

Do not be anxious about anything, but in everything,
by prayer and petition, with thanksgiving, present
your requests to God. And the peace of God,
which transcends all understanding, will guard your
hearts and your minds in Christ Jesus.

Philippians 4:6-7

I AWOKE EARLY ON THE WEDNESDAY BEFORE SURGERY AND immediately my stomach was in a knot. I wasn't tense because of the surgery itself; rather it was because there was much for me to accomplish that day. I needed to get out of bed, but my tired body and weary mind wouldn't let me. The day would begin as soon as my feet touched the floor, and I probably wouldn't stop working until late into the evening. Just a few more minutes certainly wouldn't jeopardize my list of "Things to Do." This was the day the children would be leaving to go to various homes, and most of my effort would be focused on getting them ready.

I heard the baby beginning to stir at his usual seven o'clock wake-up time. If I didn't hurry to fetch him, the other children would soon arouse from their slumber. Stumbling through the darkness, I slowly opened his creaking bedroom door. "Good morning, Samuel," I whispered with a half-smile. I was delighted to see our fifth child's adorable face but not happy about having to leave the warmth of my bed.

Mornings in our home were usually the same. If I wasn't disciplined to wake up before the children, then the day would be a little more hectic. With all that there was to do I had hoped to have risen a bit earlier. It would be an uphill battle to carry on with our routine without first having showered, dressed, and spent time alone with the Lord in prayer.

I brought Samuel to bed with me and nursed him for about twenty minutes while thinking of a new strategy to fit everything in. This would be our last day together as a family for a long time, and I didn't want the hustle and bustle of activity to put a strain on my relationship with the children. I tend to become impatient and irritable with their demands when under stress. I vowed to work hard at not letting this happen today, even if the morning didn't begin as I had wished.

Samuel let me put him back to bed without a fuss. I decided against taking a shower, hopeful that I might get one later. There was still a few loads of laundry left to do before packing all the children's suitcases.

Before heading down to the basement to throw in a load, I stopped by the kitchen and reviewed my list of chores. There was school work to gather together for Moriah and Nathan, baby items to assemble for Samuel, phone calls to make, going-away gifts to wrap for Hannah, and letters to write. A close friend asked if she could come over to visit and help me however I needed. I planned on putting her to work with some cleaning, specifically the bathrooms and the kitchen floor. My desire was to come home from a week in the hospital and not have anything to think about except for taking care of Hannah. Having a clean house certainly wasn't crucial, but I would rest easier if it had been done.

One by one the gang descended the stairs to greet me. Already I was slipping into a foul mood. Why hadn't I prioritized the day better, putting the Lord first? This was always a struggle for me, and I failed to have victory over it on a consistent basis. Today seemed to be no different, and I was frustrated with myself for not heeding the Spirit's leading. My daughter was about to undergo heart surgery, and I found more important things to do than to pray for her and our family.

The familiar story of Mary and Martha in Luke 10 is a good reminder of what God considers to be important. Jesus entered a village where a woman named Martha invited Him to fellowship at her house. Martha busied herself by waiting on Jesus while her sister, Mary, sat at His feet, listening to His teaching. Martha became annoyed at Mary's failure to see how hard she was working to serve Jesus, and she took this matter to the Lord:

Lord, don't you care that my sister has left me to do the work by myself? Tell her to help me!

"Martha, Martha," the Lord answered, "you are worried and upset about many things, but only one thing is needed. Mary has chosen what is better, and it will not be taken away from her." (Luke 10:41)

How often I had deliberately not chosen "what is better"! Again I had failed to rest at the feet of Christ and opted to busy myself with more frivolous pursuits. Instead of taking a moment to quiet myself before the Lord, I chose to make my list the priority. Would I ever learn?

My friend arrived shortly after breakfast, and, after catching up on life for a few moments, both of us plunged into our work. Moriah and Nathan sat at the kitchen table doing their school work while Hannah and Abigail spent time coloring, reading books, or playing games. Every now and then one of them would find me and ask for help. It took everything within me to patiently tolerate their requests, hoping that they would be appeased quickly and then go back to playing.

Samuel was scheduled to leave around 3 p.m., the time that Patti, Phil's sister, would be arriving. Patti and her husband, Craig, had three children of their own, between the ages of five and eleven. It had been a long time since having a baby in their home, and she was looking forward to cuddling with a little one again. I had made sure that Samuel's gear was ready first. There are so many things to pack for such a small person: clothes, diapers, baby food, bottles, bibs, toys, medicines . . . . I went over the list several times and was sure that everything Samuel needed was packed.

Patti arrived in the afternoon, and we went over Samuel's daily schedule. Being the fifth child, Samuel didn't have as strict a routine as our first babies. Much of what I instructed Patti to do was followed by, "We're flexible, so use your best judgment. After a while, you'll know what's best for him." Patti was the perfect choice to care for my precious, little boy. I had never left any of our children for this long at so young an age, but I wasn't concerned that Samuel would miss me. I expected him to thrive on the attention that he wasn't used to getting at home. Patti's enthusiasm for taking Samuel also helped me to be at ease.

I tenderly nursed Samuel one last time before saying good-bye. Moriah and Nathan doted on him with hugs and kisses. Sadly, Hannah and Abigail were sleeping soundly upstairs and didn't have the chance to do the same.

Patti had brought Hannah a gift to take with her to the hospital, but she didn't wake up in time to open it before Patti left. The thought crossed my mind to wake Hannah up so that Patti could see her one last time, but I chose to let her sleep so that more work could be done without the interruption of a demanding four year old. Again I had allowed the drive for work to interfere with the relationships between people, a decision I later regretted.

Phil arrived home from work and was just in time to see Samuel once more. As our son left home, he looked content in Aunt Patti's arms, and this made our parting more pleasant. One child gone and three to go—back to work!

Initially I had planned to make a quick dinner, but the day had gotten away from me and there was still much to do! We decided on ordering pizza to keep things simple. Hannah would enjoy this most of all, as pizza was high on her list of favorite foods. Phil went into town to pick up our dinner while I continued packing.

I'd like to write that our last family meal together was a momentous occasion as we sat around the kitchen table, sharing our feelings about the day and laughing at ourselves. Unfortunately, all I can remember was swiftly devouring my pizza and excusing myself to continue working! Rather than relish the last moments, I chose to finish the last-minute packing instead.

I know that all mothers struggle to find a balance between spending time with their children and handling the workload for the day. The cooking, school work, and laundry always needs to be done, leaving very little time for play. It wasn't as if I pushed my children out of the way so that I could watch TV or absorb myself in an enjoyable hobby. Raising a family takes much physical and mental energy, and my desire to do this well often clashed with the children's desire to spend time with me. I wrestled with this balance regularly, and it seemed that today, because of Hannah's approaching surgery, I felt this more heavily.

After a day of whirlwind activity, every item was crossed off my list, and the children were ready to go. Once we were all together in the living room, Moriah initiated the gift giving with a poem she had written for Hannah earlier that day. The children had not expressed their feelings about Hannah's surgery too often, but this poem gave me a glimpse of what was circulating through Moriah's mind.

My Dearest Hannah,
    It will be hard for me to leave you and have you go off into a hospital room to have heart surgery. Even though your constant nagging can bug me, I still will miss you this week. So I decided I would write this poem to you:

> Oh Hannah, how you can be very sweet,
> And I can't wait to meet,
> A sweet, brand-new Hannah,
> That we call "Hannah Banana."
>
> Your cute little face,
> Wants me to embrace,
> Myself all around you,
> Because I love you.

    I hope that it is not hard for you to have to go through this, but I know that it is part of God's plan. I love you.

Love,
Moriah

It is doubtful Hannah understood all that Moriah was trying to communicate, but she smiled anyway, and Moriah was proud and satisfied. The gift giving continued on.

One of Hannah's favorite characters was Strawberry Shortcake, a doll that had made a comeback from the days when I was a little girl. Knowing that Hannah would be amused with it, Moriah bought a miniature Angel Cake doll (one of Strawberry's friends) and gave it to her on behalf of the children. Moriah had guessed right—Hannah was pleased with the doll. I asked her, "Why are you getting all these gifts? Is it your birthday?"

"No," she answered as if I was ridiculously silly. "It's not my birthday!"

"Well, if it isn't your birthday, why *are* you getting all these presents?"

Hannah shrugged her shoulders and raised her eyebrows. "I don't know . . . ."

Once again I told Hannah that in two days she would be having heart surgery. We were going to the hospital where the doctors and nurses would make her heart new. I wanted Hannah to know the details about the surgery so that the unknown would not be frightening, but she never fully grasped it. Obviously, God didn't want Hannah to understand the need for heart surgery, and this belief kept us from being obsessed about her comprehension.

Hannah trusted us completely and was content to accept whatever we said was for her good. This must be what Jesus meant when He said in Matthew 18:3, *"I tell you the truth, unless you change and become like little children, you will never enter the kingdom of heaven."* Hannah exemplified the childlike faith that we are instructed from Scripture to emulate. She had faith in her earthly father's will and accepted his guidance, just as we are to trust that our heavenly Father's sovereign plan is for our best. Phil and I, as Hannah's God-given guardians on earth, sought His wisdom for how to raise her for His glory. At times we didn't always completely depend on Christ, but relied on our own efforts to train her up instead. It was a constant give-and-take surrendering, and we committed Hannah's life back to Him repeatedly.

When all the gifts were opened, Phil led the six of us in prayer, asking God to protect each child as they went away from home. We thanked God for those who agreed to care for our children and asked that each family would be given an extra measure of grace.

Upon the close of our prayer, I ran to the hall closet for the camera. "Wait right there everyone! I want to get a picture before you leave." Four smiling faces looked up at me, and I snapped a quick photo. *Would this be the last picture taken of our four children together?* I pushed this thought out of my mind and focused on helping the kids put on their shoes and coats. I refused to blemish this moment with fear of an outcome that couldn't be controlled.

With the van loaded and four children strapped in their car seats, we headed into town to drop off the kids. Moriah would be staying at the home of Eric and Wendy Corey, friends that we had met only a short time before but felt like we had known for several years. Eric and Wendy had one child, Elizabeth, almost six months in age. Moriah would enjoy being big sister to "Ellie" for a week, and Wendy was sure to appreciate an extra helper around the house. Moriah was also looking forward to spending some needed time away from the harassment of her siblings. The Coreys had big things planned for Moriah, and she anticipated never a dull moment.

Although Moriah was hoping to escape her brother and sister for a while, she wouldn't get very far without seeing them. The Calhoun family, with whom Nathan and Abigail would be staying, lived right next door to the Corey's! Ron and Kristi Calhoun were like family to us, and both had known our children since birth. With four children of their own, adding two more would certainly make life more hectic. I was so pleased with how God ideally worked out these arrangements for us. Only little Samuel would be separated from the other children, as Aunt Patti's house was an hour away in Clarkston.

Hannah traveled with us of course, and she watched while we unloaded her sisters and brothers along with all their belongings. Moriah, Nathan, and Abigail all shared a brief special moment, saying good-bye and hugging their sister. At a time like this it seemed they understood the seriousness of surgery more than we thought. Not only would the children be missing their daddy and mama for a week, but Hannah would be missed, too. Her absence would not go unnoticed.

With just one child in our full-size van, we started on the short drive back to our home in the countryside. It was almost 8 p.m., and we had an eight o'clock pre-operative testing appointment scheduled the next morning in Ann Arbor. This meant we had to be awake by 5 a.m. and out the door no later than six. I still had some packing to finish for Phil and me but decided it could wait until we returned home on Thursday afternoon.

Just after arriving to our quiet, empty house, I immediately informed Hannah that we had another surprise waiting for her. "What is it?" she asked curiously.

"Come into the living room and see!" I was so excited to watch the look on Hannah's face as she opened our gifts. They were "wrapped" in the plastic bags from the store where I purchased them. (Wrapping her gifts was one of those items on my list that was overlooked for the sake of more urgent matters!) Hannah's excitement to see what was inside each bag made up for the poor packaging.

The first surprise was a Strawberry Shortcake rag doll. "Mama bought her for you to take to the hospital tomorrow," I said. "You can show Strawberry all the places that you have to go!"

The doll was just the right size and fit perfectly into her small hands. Hannah demonstrated her pleasure by seeking Phil's approval: "Look, Daddy!"

"Wow, Hannah! Strawberry Shortcake! I like her!" It didn't matter what Phil said to Hannah, but how he said it was important to her. His excitement made her light up even more.

"Now open your next present," I encouraged Hannah. "I think you're really going to like it!"

I affectionately referred to Hannah as our "character child." She cherished many girl-loved characters such as Barbie, Angelina Ballerina, and most of all, Cinderella. When Moriah was Hannah's age I steered away from owning any toys, clothes, or books with these characters, out of concern that she might become obsessed. Seems silly now to think that I worried so much about this! But Hannah, born four years later, was given more freedom in this area as we lightened up a little.

Although we didn't spoil Hannah with material things, we did enjoy splurging now and then on a gift we knew would bring her happiness. The present she was about to open was just such a gift, chosen especially by me, to bring joy during this uncertain time.

"What is it?" I asked, fully knowing but wanting to hear it from her.

She pulled it from the bag in a heap and tried holding it up to get a better look. "Here, let me help you, Hannah," volunteered Phil.

I didn't wait for Hannah to guess what it was on her own. "Look!" I exclaimed. "It's a princess nightgown with Cinderella, Snow White, and Sleeping Beauty!"

Hannah sat quiet for a moment as she looked over all the princesses on the purple silk nightgown with long sheer sleeves. "What do you think?" I asked.

"I like it! Can I go put it on?"

"Absolutely! Mama bought this for you to wear tonight and tomorrow at bedtime. Let's get your clothes off and see how it looks!"

A perfect fit in size and a perfect match for Hannah's sweet spirit. It was as if the nightgown had been made just for her. I'm not sure who was more proud, Hannah or me!

Carrying the new doll and dressed in her nightgown, Hannah and I went upstairs to get ready for bed. "Tomorrow is a long day and we all need to be well rested."

"I don't want to go to bed!" Hannah pouted. "Mama, can I watch a movie?" she asked with a sweet but manipulative expression. She sure knew how to play on my sympathies!

Every bit of good sense within me told me to say no. To avoid looking like the "Mean Mama," I slyly passed the weight of this decision off to Phil. "What do you think, Daddy?"

Without a moment's hesitation, Phil answered, "Let's watch *Cinderella!* Come on, Hannah! Climb into our bed. We'll even make popcorn!" Hannah's spell on Daddy was stronger than I thought. How easily he was charmed by her!

As Hannah sat up in our bed, sharing a big bowl of popcorn with Daddy, *Cinderella* played on the television. It was Hannah's favorite movie, and she never grew tired of watching it.

It was 10 p.m. when the movie ended. Hannah should have been in bed hours before, especially since we had to be up early the next day. I should have been furious with Phil for allowing this, but seeing Hannah's joy as she cuddled with him made all my regrets about the late hour melt away.

"OK, Hannah. Now it's really time for bed," I said. "Off you go, Young Lady! Hey, you get to sleep in this big bed all by yourself!"

"Abigail's at the Calhoun's?" asked Hannah as if needing assurance.

"Yes. You won't see Abigail, Moriah, Nathan, or Samuel for a while. Remember when Mama told you about going to the hospital for heart surgery?"

"Are they going to cut me?" asked Hannah unbelievingly.

"Yes, but you will be sleeping and won't feel anything. The doctors are going to make your heart better so that you can run and play without getting tired."

"I don't like that!"

"No, Daddy and I don't like it either, but it's what we have to do, Sweetheart. Let Mama pray for you, OK?"

"OK, Mama." She was so trusting; so accepting. Her strength in this trial made me feel weaker and more nervous. What did she see in me that was worth putting all her faith in?

"Lord Jesus, tomorrow is going to be a long day. Please help us drive to the hospital safely, and help Hannah to be brave. We know that You will be with her every step of the way. And as always, if it be Your will, heal Hannah's heart. There is still time. Give her a long life so that she can speak of Your marvelous works and bring glory to Your name. Amen."

"Good night, Hannah. See you bright and early tomorrow morning."

"Night, Mama. I love you."

"Love you too, Darling."

♥♥

We managed to get out of the house as planned on Thursday morning. All three of us were tired, but the grogginess wore off before arriving at the hospital. Since Hannah's pre-operative testing promised to make for a long day, we needed as much energy as possible to get through all six hours.

The first stop on Hannah's journey of testing was the radiology department for a chest X-ray. While waiting to be called, another family came into the room and sat across from us. The parents looked to be about the same age as Phil and me, but I wasn't certain about the age of their son. I was drawn to gaze at the tender interaction of these parents with their dearly-loved child. The young boy's disabilities confined him permanently to a wheelchair. A tracheotomy had been placed in his throat to help him breathe, and he required oxygen. It was obvious that this child needed continuous care as provided for by his parents, who probably didn't get much respite time away. I leaned over and whispered to Phil, "Looking at them really puts our situation in perspective, doesn't it?"

Considering all that we had gone through with Hannah's illnesses and surgeries, putting our circumstances in perspective always helped us to cope. Hannah's disorder, while trying at times, could have been much worse. No matter what happened, there was always someone else who had experienced a trial more devastating. It helped to realize that we were not alone. There were multitudes of parents like us who daily managed the needs and limitations of their special-needs child. Aligning our perspective had definitely caused us to be thankful for what God had chosen to give, and we realized what a privilege it was to nurture such a precious child for His glory.

Waiting for the X-ray didn't take long. Hannah was cheerful until we walked into the exam room. Before anyone even touched her, the tears started flowing like a faucet! "Hannah, what's wrong?" I asked.

In protest, the crying became louder. "There's nothing to be scared of, Hannah. The nurse is just going to take a picture of your heart. It won't hurt at all."

The nurse joined in with my reassurance, but Hannah was not persuaded. In our experience, we had found that the best way to handle Hannah's apprehension was to carry on with the procedure and not coddle her fears. If I waited for her to settle down, we might have been in the radiology department all day! It was best to gently proceed and get the X-ray over with as soon as possible.

Hannah fussed the entire time, and I shook my head in disbelief. *Is this what I should expect for the remainder of today's testing?* I asked myself. *If a harmless procedure can create this type of response, what would Hannah be like tomorrow?*

The nurse was gracious to Hannah, praising her for being "brave." Hannah stopped crying as she was helped down from the X-ray table and handed a sticker. "Can we go now, Mama?"

"Almost. We have to wait right here to see if the pictures turned out."

Fortunately the X-rays didn't need retaking. Hannah skipped happily back to the waiting room where she gave Daddy a full report of the previous trauma.

Our next pre-op destination was the cardiology department where Hannah would undergo an echocardiogram and EKG of her heart. Phil stayed in the waiting area while I took Hannah back to the ultrasound exam room. At the sight of the machinery, Hannah started to tear up, and her bottom lip quivered with fright. I couldn't believe it! Ever since infancy, Hannah had many tests performed, all without painful incident. Couldn't she reason that these tests, like those given many times before, would not be distressing?

As always, I took a matter-of-fact posture towards Hannah's anxiety. "Let's get you up on the table, Hannah. Mama will lay with you." Noticing a television nearby I asked, "Would you like to watch TV?"

The sonographer helped us choose a channel that held Hannah's interest long enough to distract her. Hannah instantly calmed down and became fixated on the screen. She sucked her thumb and stroked her blanket for further comfort. How relieved I was! This was the first time that I actually could thank God for television!

An hour passed by before the tests were complete. Hannah continued to be preoccupied with the TV programs until the very end. The sonographer directed us back to the waiting room where we would wait to see the cardiologist. Hannah kept herself busy by silently reading books and appeared to be beyond the initial fearfulness brought on by the testing.

The lunch hour was approaching, and the receptionist encouraged us to take a break before meeting with the cardiologist who was late in coming. With the suggestion of lunch made in front of Hannah, it would have been impossible to wait. She had already devoured the graham crackers and juice provided by the receptionist and was still hungry. Hannah loved eating, especially if it involved dining out in a restaurant. There was no denying her appetite! We decided that it was a good time to stop for lunch or else we might never hear the end of Hannah's pleading.

At the University of Michigan Hospital complex, there were only two places to eat lunch—the cafeteria and Wendy's. We decided that going to Wendy's would be quicker than the cafeteria as there were fewer options and more economical prices. Hannah was pleased with our decision: "Yea! Wendy's!" Phil and I walked on either side of her through the long hallways, picking her up on the count of three and swinging her feet into the air. Hannah was in her glory, having the attention of Daddy and Mama all to herself.

Hannah chose to eat chicken tenders with fries, and she relished every bite ever so slowly. Phil and I both finished eating before her, and, while we enjoyed Hannah's company, we continually implored her to hurry. Hannah would smile and giggle, take another bite of food, and then become distracted again by her surroundings. She certainly loved to be around people and found them interesting to watch. Of course, it didn't help when those people waved back at Hannah and commented, "Isn't she cute?"

On our way back from lunch we stopped at the front desk of the Med Inn, a hotel connected right to the hospital. Because inclement weather threatened to make driving difficult the following morning, we thought it would be wise to secure a room for Thursday evening in order to avoid a long, hazardous drive.

Presently, the hotel didn't have any rooms available, but it looked promising if we put our names on the waiting list. We added our names, making us the fifth family in line for a vacant room. If God meant for us to stay overnight, we were confident that a room would become open. Until then, there wasn't anything else we could do except to trust in Him to provide.

Back at the cardiologist's office, we waited only a short time before seeing the doctor. She reviewed the results of the morning's tests and asked if we had any more questions, which we did not.

Next, a Child Life Specialist came into the room and talked with us about what we could expect concerning Hannah's recovery. She encouraged us to visit the playrooms during our hospital stay in order to help Hannah heal more rapidly. The specialist gave Hannah a stuffed doll, hand-sewn for children facing surgery by a group of women. The doll was dressed in a hospital gown and didn't have eyes, a nose, or mouth. Hannah was told to draw the doll's face with a marker and carry her along as a constant companion during her hospitalization. She seemed to be fond of the doll at first, but quickly became disinterested, finding the chairs more fun to climb under. Hannah had always been challenged to keep busy with one task for any length of time. Apparently not even a new doll could make her sit still!

The last stop for the day was the most dreaded for all— drawing blood. The medical staff was wise to save "pokes" for the end, as it was certain to cause panic within Hannah. I was upfront about the procedure, telling Hannah that the nurse would be using a needle to draw blood from her arm. She whimpered but went right on playing with the toys in her backpack, unphased by my explanation. *Maybe this won't be so bad,* I thought.

It was our turn to take a seat in the chair. Hannah sat on my lap and remained calm until the nurse tied the elastic band around her upper arm. This must have reminded Hannah of the last blood draw just two weeks before. She immediately began to cry, observing the nurse's every move through big, watery eyes. Then, when the nurse brought out the needle, that was it for Hannah! She wailed at the injustice, and I tried to quiet her sobs: "It's OK, Hannah. It will all be over soon. It'll only hurt for a second."

The nurse was very skilled and was able to draw Hannah's blood on the first try. She taped a cotton ball on Hannah's arm and awarded her courage with a sticker. (By now we had quite a collection!) Hannah's distressed countenance immediately changed to joy. "You were so brave, Hannah!" I told her. "You held so still! Let's go tell Daddy how brave you were!"

We ran out of the lab and found Daddy waiting in the hallway. "Look, Daddy!" exclaimed Hannah as she held up her arm. "I was brave!"

Phil laughed and took Hannah up into his arms. "Let me see—wow! You were brave! I'm so proud of you!" Glancing at me over Hannah's head, Phil silently mouthed, "How was it?"

"She cried but held real still," I whispered. "It was cute to watch."

"Guess what, Hannah. It's time to go home now! You're all done!"

"Yea!" answered Hannah. It was now 2 p.m., and we were starting to feel the exhaustion set in. Although we were weary,

Hannah's energy level had turned up a few notches. In her excitement to leave the hospital, she pulled us all the way to the car.

Not surprisingly, Hannah fell asleep on the ride home. I tried to keep my eyes open so that Phil would have some company while driving, but sleep won out. Phil was left to his own thoughts, many of which focused on surgery.

Overall, the pre-operative testing went perfectly. God had chosen to answer yes to our first request from a long list of prayers. With thanksgiving and praise to the God who holds all things in His hands, we prepared ourselves for the next step.

"Mama, play a game with me," begged Hannah for the third time. We were home from the hospital, and I went right to work finishing up the last-minute details.

"Hannah, I told you that when I finished writing these letters I'd play Scoops with you. Why don't you color a picture next to me while I work?"

Phil and I sat at the kitchen table writing letters to Moriah and Nathan. It seemed to be a good idea when I had thought of it earlier in the week. I wanted Moriah and Nathan to open a letter from Phil or me each day while we were away. Since we planned to be gone for one full week, this meant that we had seven letters to write for each child. So far I had only written a few of the notes, and I was anxious to finish them before leaving. Phil was less impressed with my idea but went along with it to appease me. "How many of these letters do we have to write," he asked in exasperation.

I was hesitant to be completely honest for fear that he would give up midway through. "Just keep writing. We're almost done."

"I'd rather be spending this time playing with Hannah. The kids won't know what they're missing if we don't do this."

I sighed and gave Phil "the look." He reached for another piece of paper and wrote fast and furiously. My devotion between Hannah and the other children was torn. I could see Phil's point in wanting to spend every last minute with Hannah, yet it would be at least a week before we had any physical contact with Moriah and Nathan who would surely miss us. "Just keep the letters short," I encouraged Phil. "I only want them to know that we're thinking of them every day. It doesn't have to be elaborate."

While writing Phil said, "We should call the Med Inn to see if our name has moved up on the waiting list. It's getting close to six o' clock, and I want to know ahead of time if there a possibility of us leaving home tonight."

"I'll do that right after finishing this letter." A quick call to the hotel revealed that we were now third on the list.

"Have you decided where we should go for dinner tonight, Hannah?" I asked.

"Are we going soon?"

"Not for a little while yet. We have a few more things to do here at home, and then we'll leave."

"Is Moriah coming, too? Is Nathan or Abigail?"

"Nope! Just you, and me, and Daddy!"

"Not Samuel?"

"Samuel is staying at Aunt Patti's, remember?"

"Oh! Are we going soon?"

That was the fourth time Hannah had made this inquiry in the last hour. Eating dinner out was indeed the highlight of her day! As a mother of five children who didn't always get along, I was pleased to hear that she wanted to include her siblings also. Hannah enjoyed spending time with just Daddy and Mama, but there was something special about being with them, too. They were missed already.

With the letters finally finished, I went to work packing our clothes and also a bag for Hannah. She would need pajamas, clothes for the day of surgery, shoes, socks, hair supplies, and of course, her blanket. I also included a surprise that Hannah would see on the day of her discharge from the hospital—a Barbie blanket sleeper! This would keep her warm and comfortable for the drive back to Williamston.

I looked forward to dressing Hannah in those pajamas, as it would mean the end of our ordeal. Heart surgery would be behind us. Hannah would be healthy, strong, and energetic. And most importantly, God would be praised for answering our prayers the way we had hoped.

Just one more task before spending time with Hannah: updating the Website that we created to communicate the details of her surgery and recovery. I wanted to inform our prayer warriors about the day's events and offer praise to God for answering their prayers. I also asked our friends to pray that a room would open up for us at the hotel.

Hannah continued to wait patiently for Phil and I to finish our duties. At last we were able to play the long-awaited game of Scoops, undisturbed by the demands of work. It was so liberating to enjoy Hannah without thinking of everything that needed to be done.

As we played the game, a love for Hannah welled up within me like never before. I was her mom; she was my daughter. Bone of my bone and flesh of my flesh. This little person who sat next to me had been made by God and was given to me. I was responsible for her while here on earth. While this should have produced a weight on our time together, I experienced the opposite. I was free! Free to enjoy her fully; free to love her completely. Worry and anxiety went away as I realized that God, who loved Hannah the most, was always looking out for her.

I can't recall a feeling like that in all my days of parenting. God's grace gave me the boost I needed to carry on without the burden of wondering whether she would live or die. All I could do was take pleasure in being with her for that moment. I didn't have to worry about tomorrow, for tomorrow had enough trouble of its own (Matthew 6:34).

"Mama," shrieked Hannah, "it's your turn!"

"Look at all that ice cream on your plate! You little piggy!"

"No, Mama. You're the little pig!"

"I think Daddy is the little pig!"

We laughed uncontrollably as Hannah latched on to the phrase "little pig." She continued to name call all throughout the game until Phil finally put a stop to it. It seems unthinkable that our sweet Hannah could actually be disrespectful, but by the way she repeatedly taunted Phil, she had come awfully close. I certainly didn't help the situation; my laughter only cajoled Hannah to keep it going. Now it was Phil's turn to give me "the look." I bit my lower lip to conceal the laughter and tried to focus on playing the game.

The phone rang and we checked the Caller ID to see who it was. "It's from Ann Arbor," Phil called out. "Same number as earlier in the day."

Upon arriving home, we had checked our messages to see who phoned. Around 12 p.m., someone tried to contact us from Ann Arbor, but they didn't leave a message. This was strange—at noon we were in the hospital. Why couldn't they have looked for us there?

I was distracted with Hannah and didn't hear Phil's conversation. He hung up the phone with a concerned look. "That was the hospital calling. The surgery has been bumped from seven-thirty to twelve o'clock. There's been an emergency, and we've been rescheduled."

"No!" I exclaimed. "Why didn't they tell us this when we were there today?"

"I didn't ask that. Thankfully, Hannah was the only surgery scheduled for tomorrow. If there happens to be another emergency, we'll be moved to a totally different day."

I had feared this from the beginning. All my effort to get to this point might have been for nothing! This wasn't what we wanted, but since everything is ordained by God, including the time set for Hannah's surgery, we continued to trust Him for the perfect timing.

"Will we still go to the hotel tonight?" I asked. "The weather will probably have improved by the late morning."

"If a room becomes available, we'll go. That way we won't have to worry about it."

The phone rang again. Phil had the cordless receiver in hand and he answered it on the first ring. It was the hotel, calling to tell us that our room was now ready.

"We'll take it." Phil gave the receptionist our credit card number to hold the room since we would be arriving late. I started upstairs and began bringing our suitcases down. This was it!

In the midst of our rush to load the car, Hannah asked once more, "Are we going to dinner now?"

I could finally reply in the affirmative: "Yes! And we're also going to the hotel tonight! Just you, and me, and Daddy. You'll get to stay in the hotel all by yourself with just us!"

Hannah was delighted. I wished that we had made this much fuss over her during a time other than before heart surgery. It appeared as if we were luring her to the hospital using "fun" as the bait. Hannah still seemed clueless about the surgery. I wondered what she would think tomorrow as this excitement culminated in her separation from us. In a way it felt like we were deceiving her.

I updated the Website one last time from home, asking for prayer regarding the postponement of surgery and thanking the Lord for providing a room. The next time I planned on posting to the site would be after saying good-bye to Hannah just before surgery.

Phil stopped me at the back door before walking out. He grabbed my shoulders and looked me straight in the eye. "Sandy, whatever happens, please don't have any regrets. Trust that the way this works out is the way it was meant to be. No regrets, OK?"

"Sure. No regrets," I answered tentatively. "I have always believed that God is in control." Why was he telling me this now? Did Phil sense a bad outcome for the surgery? I didn't have the courage to ask. *Just get in the car,* I told myself. *Don't dwell on it.*

As the car drove down the driveway, the three of us shouted, "Good-bye, House! See you in a week!" This was something the Dufrin family always said if we were planning to be away for an extended time. It was as if our house was a member of the family, too!

Hannah couldn't decide on her own where she wanted to eat, so Phil gave her a suggestion. "What about the Cracker Barrel?" he asked.

"Yea! Cacka Barro!" I found it humorous that Phil would propose his favorite restaurant. Evidently both father and daughter shared a fondness for The Cracker Barrel that Mama didn't know anything about!

Hannah ordered macaroni and cheese from the children's menu, and she quickly consumed the food. The time was nearing 8 p.m., and naturally we were famished.

Phil got up to pay the check, and I stared at Hannah sitting across from me. "What?" she asked with a "stop looking at me" tone in her voice.

"You are so beautiful, Hannah."

"Noooo." Hannah always pretended not to enjoy compliments, but I think that she secretly enjoyed the praise.

I wanted to gaze at my daughter's big brown eyes and long, wavy hair for a few more hours, but obviously our schedule wouldn't allow it and neither would Hannah. Why hadn't I taken the time to intently look at her more often?

Phil came back to the table and helped put Hannah's coat on. "Off to the hotel, Hannah!" he exclaimed.

"We go now?" she asked in a hopeful tone. Hannah had patiently waited all day for this very moment.

"Yes!" I answered enthusiastically. "Let's get in the car!"

After another thirty minutes of driving, we found a parking spot close to the elevator without difficulty. There was a luggage cart nearby, so Phil didn't have to carry our suitcases through the long maze of hallways. Since there was no outside entrance to the Med Inn, we had to walk all the way through the hospital to get to the hotel lobby. Due to the late hour, we only passed a handful of people which was much different than earlier. Hannah enjoyed running ahead, looking back, and then waiting for us to catch up.

The hotel was a little run down but clean. Our room was connected to the same floor of the Pediatric Cardiac Intensive Care Unit; it would only be a two-minute walk to Hannah's hospital room. Hannah raced through the door and quickly scanned the furnishings: two double beds, a small table with chairs, and a television.

"What do you think, Hannah?" asked Phil as he began carrying our bags inside.

Hannah was too busy trying to climb into the chair to comment. She plopped down on the seat, crossed her legs, laid back, and grinned.

"She looks comfortable!" I laughed. "Guess she approves!"

Since we were going to be staying there for a while, I put our clothes in the dresser and closet so that we weren't living out of a suitcase for a week. Phil and Hannah cuddled together on the bed, flipping through the channels on the TV.

"OK, Young Lady. That's enough TV for tonight!" Phil said as he clicked off the television using the remote control. "You need to get to bed!"

It was close to 10 p.m.—another late night! I helped Hannah into her princess nightgown and brushed her teeth. She crawled into bed and pulled the blankets up to her chest. The Strawberry Shortcake doll I had given her yesterday was in her hands. She

nestled into the pillow and prepared herself for kisses from Phil and I on the cheek.

"Good night, Sweet Girl," I whispered while stroking her head. "Sleep well. Tomorrow is your big day, and you need your rest."

Hannah fell asleep a few minutes after we turned off the lamp light. The possibility of this being the last time I would tuck her into bed hadn't even occurred to me once. I was too tired and focused on getting into bed myself. But had I remembered, Phil would certainly have been without a sleeping partner for the night as I would have slept with Hannah instead, holding her tightly from behind, smelling her hair, and kissing her endlessly the whole night through.

No regrets. Not tonight and not ever. God *is* in control.

In moments like this we do not question God or blame Him for taking us down this hard road. How could we? He has blessed us far more than imaginable but not by giving us five beautiful children, a faithful group of family and friends, or material things. He has blessed us with HOPE. And that hope can only be found in Christ. If He chooses to take Hannah to be with Him, we will see her again one day. We are completely confident of His grace and will not doubt.

We are privileged to go through this so that Christ may be exalted. I know to some that may not sound real, but when I look at what God has done in our lives, there is nothing more certain.

FEBRUARY 7, 2004
4:27 P.M.

4

A Time to Die

I tell you the truth, unless a kernel
of wheat falls to the ground and dies,
it remains only a single seed. But if
it dies, it produces many seeds.

John 12:24

IN THE WAITING ROOM ON THE FIFTH FLOOR, PHIL AND I camped out in the back corner, trying to keep ourselves busy. The room itself had a dual purpose, serving as the surgical waiting area and as a room for parents of hospitalized patients to unwind and rest. I wasn't trying to infringe on people's privacy, but every conversation could be easily overheard no matter how engrossed in my knitting project I tried to be. It didn't take long to figure out the personal stories of each family. It appeared that we were the only parents waiting for our child during surgery. I quietly kept to myself, hoping that no one would start up a conversation with me. I wasn't in the mood to be sociable.

Phil was having more success concentrating on reading than me; I read the same paragraph over and over until finally giving up altogether. Every so often he would stop reading and say, "Listen to this!" I would look up from my knitting briefly to catch his eye and acknowledge that I was listening. He was reading the autobiography of John G. Paton, missionary to the South Sea Islands. Although our situations were very different, the quotes Phil read to me strangely applied to our current trial. We were both amazed by Paton's faith which never wavered in spite of the losses he experienced in life. It was evident that God had deliberately placed this book in Phil's hands to help prepare us for the events of the next twenty-four hours.

"Hannah Dufrin?" a nurse called out from the doorway of the waiting room. It had been less than an hour since she was taken away in the red wagon. We had been told that a nurse would report on Hannah's progress midway through the surgery. "No news is good news," they had assured us. "If something goes wrong, we will come let you know right away." Imagine our alarm at receiving an update so soon!

Our hearts stopped and we held our breath. What had already gone wrong? As the nurse walked closer, I tried to read the expression on her face. After years of delivering news to nervous, waiting families, she had learned to keep a straight face so as not to mislead the recipients. She came within six feet of our chairs, then stopped. We looked up at her with wide, suspenseful eyes.

"We've made the incision," the nurse stated very matter-of-factly. By her intonation, I sensed that she had reported everything, and there wasn't anything more we could ask. Needless to say, we were relieved that all seemed to be going well. She promised to give us an update every hour or so.

We decided that this would be a good time to eat a late lunch. Neither of us were very hungry, but eating might help the time go faster until the next report. On the way down to the cafeteria, we stopped at the computer to post an update on the Website. Literally hundreds of people would be checking the site throughout the afternoon to get the latest news of Hannah's progress. We wanted them to be adequately informed so that they could pray more specifically for Hannah during the surgery.

Back in the waiting room I continued to knit, and Phil plugged away on the Paton biography. Around 3:45 p.m., the nurse who spoke to us an hour before walked into the room with the same expressionless countenance. I wasn't nearly so alarmed since we were expecting an update this time.

She told us that the surgery had gone well so far. Dr. Bove's original plan was to go into Hannah's heart through the aortic valve. However, the thick wall of the left ventricle appeared to be in a tricky spot. Because Dr. Bove could not reach it from the aorta, he had to make a hole between the left and right ventricles. This type of setback was not unusual, nor would it make Hannah's recovery more difficult. Quite often the exact surgical procedure was hard to know for certain until the surgeon opened the chest.

Hearing this news didn't cause Phil and I to become more anxious. Reality should have told us that our daughter's body was now being kept alive by a heart and lung machine. Surgeons were performing open heart surgery. They had made incisions on her heart. Yet in spite of these harsh truths, the whole experience truly didn't seem real.

Each time a report on Hannah's progress was given, it seemed like the nurse was talking about someone other than our daughter. Surely someone else's child was in that operating room. Less than two hours before I had held Hannah on my lap and felt her heart beating with my hand. Now her heart no longer beat on its own, and the surgeon's hands were physically touching her heart instead. Perhaps our dreamlike feelings were God's way of keeping us from being fearful. After all, if it isn't your child they are talking about, what need is there to be worried?

At 4:36 p.m., the nurse came out for the last time to tell us that the surgery was complete, and the surgeons were closing Hannah's chest. These were the only details she could give. Dr. Bove would speak with us about the specifics of the surgery around 5 p.m. Hannah would be wheeled from recovery to her room in the Intensive Care Unit at 6 p.m., and then we would be allowed to visit her. I was a little nervous at the thought of seeing Hannah for the first time after surgery. Although we had been well acquainted with tubes and machines, I still wasn't sure what to expect. Heart surgery was in a class all by itself, much different from RSV and other respiratory illnesses.

Phil and I breathed a sigh of relief. Hannah's surgery appeared to be successful; the nurse gave us no indication that anything had gone wrong. Dr. Bove echoed the success when he came up to talk with us at 5:30 p.m. He began by saying that Hannah was recovering well, but the surgery didn't quite go as planned. The thickness of the heart wall required him to remove more muscle than expected, thereby leaving the wall too thin and weak. Dr. Bove decided it would be best to cut right through the wall and patch it with Gore-tex (a durable, waterproof fabric used mainly in outerwear and footwear). The muscle would then grow right around the Gore-tex to form a permanent, strong wall. Being assured that this would not complicate Hannah's overall heart function, we weren't too concerned about this news.

Hannah's heart appeared to be making sporadic attempts at pumping on its own. The conductive tissue, which receives messages from the brain and tells the heart to beat, might have been damaged during the surgery. Because of this injury, Hannah's heart could not pump without the assistance of a pacemaker. Dr. Bove told us that he wouldn't be surprised if Hannah needed a pacemaker for the rest of her life. This outcome isn't what we wanted for Hannah, but just knowing that our daughter survived the surgery overshadowed this worry. Having a pacemaker would require an adjustment in our care for her, but this was a small sacrifice to make on our part.

Our emotions upon hearing the results of Hannah's surgery are summarized best in the Website update, written by Phil:

> Mere words can't describe how we feel. We know that there is still a long road ahead, but the emotions after hearing that the surgery is finished and successful is overwhelming . . . . God has blessed us far more than we can comprehend. To simply know Hannah for four years was privilege undeserved. Now the opportunity to enjoy her more as she grows is humbling. You may not understand how I could suggest such a thing, but let me assure you, Christ has shown us a glimpse of Himself and we are undone.

It was the Lord's will that Hannah's life was sustained through heart surgery. How thankful we were that He had allowed us more time to raise her for His glory. God had given us the privilege of being Hannah's parents for a little while longer, entrusting one of His fragile little children to our care. We felt both relieved and rewarded.

"Hannah, it's Mama. Can you hear me, Sweetheart?"

"She can hear you," said the nurse. "Just keep talking even if she doesn't respond."

"Hannah, can you open your eyes? Look at Mama. I'm over here, Hannah."

We had been at Hannah's bedside for almost an hour. The nervousness I felt before seeing her was completely gone now. She looked better than I ever expected; her color was good, and she was trying to wake up a little to see us. Every now and then Hannah would open her eyes slightly and turn her head in the direction of our voices. I could tell that she recognized our faces.

A few times Hannah tried reaching up with her right hand to pull out the breathing tube. It was obviously irritating her throat and she looked uncomfortable. "Keep your hand down, Hannah," I gently encouraged her. "They'll be taking it out soon."

Even in her weakness, Hannah persisted to grasp for the tube, and I had to restrain her from pulling it out altogether. It hurt me more to watch Hannah suffer, and if possible I would have endured the pain in her place. Speaking soothing words into Hannah's ear was the only way I could comfort her. I was a helpless bystander, unable to do anything except trust the nurses who knew how to best alleviate Hannah's suffering.

There were several tubes coming in and out of Hannah's body. Whitney, Hannah's nurse, took the time to explain the purpose for each one. It was amazing to watch her work. She was so calm and confident while caring for Hannah. Phil and I appreciated how Whitney explained each medical procedure. She patiently answered all of our questions and didn't mind us scrutinizing her every move. This was further confirmation that Mott Hospital was the right place to be.

We didn't feel the urge to be constantly near Hannah's bedside, and we were always within minutes if we had to get back to her quickly. Our confidence in the treatment she received helped us to let go a little. We also realized that never leaving Hannah's side wouldn't be best for either her or us. As the days progressed she would want our comforting presence much more. It was better that we took the time to eat and sleep so that we were well rested and physically able to give Hannah the attention she required.

Because of the nurses' shift change, we were asked to leave the room while the outgoing nurse gave report to the incoming nurse. Hannah shared her room with another child—a two-month-old baby—and in order to maintain patient privacy, we couldn't be present as the nurses discussed his care. This was the perfect opportunity to make ourselves eat. Now that Hannah had made it through the worst, our anxiety had subsided and we actually felt more hungry.

Before heading down to Wendy's, we stopped by the computer and posted another update. In addition to informing our friends and relatives about Hannah's current status, we asked them to pray that the respirator tube would be taken out soon and without complication. The pacemaker was still a concern, so we also asked for prayer that Hannah's heart would start beating on its own.

Messages of support from our prayer warriors started to pour into the Website. We enjoyed reading the postings and rejoiced with those who were also relieved at the success of her surgery. Phil and I had been without company all day (which was what we preferred), and the waiting was tiresome at times. Yet because of the communication we had with others through the Website, we never felt truly alone. It also saved us many hours of talking on the phone! Typically when information gets passed from one person to another, the end result sounds nothing like the initial message. But since everyone who connected to the Website read the same message as posted directly by us, there was no chance for Hannah's progress to become distorted or exaggerated.

Upon returning from dinner, Whitney told us that Hannah had developed a slight fever which was quite common within the first twenty-four hours following surgery. She also vomited twice, most likely due to the anesthetic. These factors, in addition to a slightly lower blood pressure, caused the doctors to keep Hannah on the ventilator. More sedatives were given so that she would be still and not try to pull out the tube. The time was now 9 p.m., and Hannah would be completely unconscious for the rest of the night, oblivious that we were near her bedside. Phil and I decided to go back to our room and sleep. Hannah would need us more the next day, and we wanted to be completely rested.

How could sitting in a waiting room all day be so tiring? The stress of surgery made me more exhausted than I ever thought possible.

There were two double beds in our hotel room. "Phil, would you be offended if I slept in the other bed tonight?" I asked.

"Not at all. I was thinking the same thing," Phil answered, relieved that he didn't have to ask me this first. Preferring a sound night sleep, Phil slept in one bed, and I collapsed in the other. Even though the bed was quite uncomfortable, I had no trouble falling asleep once my head hit the pillow. The telephone and pager stayed silent through the night. I slept soundly and didn't wake up until just after seven o'clock the next morning.

෴

At 7:05 the morning of February 7, 2004, Phil posted this message on the Website:

> I have been thinking quite a bit about some verses that I have been studying recently. Ephesians 1:3 says, *"Praise be to the God and Father of our Lord Jesus Christ, who has blessed us in the heavenly realms with every spiritual blessing in Christ."* Whether life or death, pleasure or pain, happiness or sorrow, we have already received every spiritual blessing there is to be found under the heavens in Christ. Not to dismiss such things as pain and sorrow, but what joy there is to know that when this short life has come to an end, eternity without pain and sorrow and with joy everlasting is promised us in Christ. He disciplines us because He loves us and we are His (Hebrews 12:6-11), and all is intended for our good (Romans 8:28).

Phil has always been an early riser, and this morning was no exception. Understandably he was anxious to see Hannah as soon as possible. I awoke to the sound of our room door opening, and the light from the hallway caused my eyes to squint in pain.

Phil entered the room carrying his usual Styrofoam cup of morning coffee. "Where did you just come from?" I groggily asked. My assumption was that he had only gone down to the hotel lobby to partake of their measly continental breakfast.

"I went to see Hannah. She's doing great!"

Immediately I sat up, fully alert. "Tell me everything!" I demanded.

"The night went well. She still has a slight fever, but her breathing is excellent and they expect to take her off the ventilator sometime around nine o'clock this morning. The nurse commented on how much Hannah moves around. Most kids are in so much pain that they have no interest in moving. Either her senses are dulled or she is one tough little girl!"

"We both know the answer to that!" I jumped in proudly.

"Hannah kept telling me that she was hungry. That's a good sign!"

"She must be feeling better then. When can we see her again?"

"The nurses change shifts at seven-thirty. We can go back at eight-thirty and stay with her for the whole morning."

"Great news! I'll get up right away and shower. Let's be ready to go at exactly eight-thirty."

"Sounds good. Would you like me to go down and bring you up something to eat for breakfast?"

"Please, if you don't mind."

By 8:30 a.m. we were back at Hannah's bedside. The new nurse, Jackie, was taking care of Hannah and ultimately of us, too. Like Whitney, she patiently answered all of our questions and explained everything she did to care for Hannah. Phil and I pulled up two chairs next to the bed and waited for the cardiologist to give his approval to take out the breathing tube. Hannah was still completely unconscious and unaware of our presence. Feeling more at ease today than yesterday, I pulled out a magazine and had some success with reading. Phil continued reading the Paton biography, stopping to comment on the text from time to time.

A little after 9 a.m., the cardiologist called and gave his consent to take Hannah off the ventilator, but we were still waiting for the respiratory therapist to arrive. Jackie explained that before taking out the breathing tube, the therapist would turn off the ventilator for an hour to see how Hannah responded without assistance. If she was able to breathe well on her own, then the tube could be removed. It was better to run this one-hour trial first because once the tube was taken out, it would be very difficult to put back in, especially in the event of an emergency. The doctors wanted to be absolutely sure that Hannah could breathe on her own without the ventilator before taking this big step.

After the cardiologist phoned, we noticed a concerned look on Jackie's face. "Is everything OK?" I asked.

Without looking away from the monitor, Jackie answered, "Hannah's blood pressure keeps dropping a little."

"What does that mean?"

"She seems to be fine now, but we'll keep watching it closely." I knew this was Jackie's universal, pat answer given to mothers like me who began to sense that something wasn't quite right. Throughout Hannah's many hospitalizations, Phil and I had learned that the medical community doesn't like to unduly alarm parents unless there was a significant reason. Many times they just weren't sure what was going on and refrained from confessing their uncertainty for fear of stirring up anxiety in parents.

By 12:30 in the afternoon, Hannah's condition had worsened. The fever was now being treated with antibiotics. Her blood pressure continued to drop without known cause. Phil and I stood in the hallway outside Hannah's room as the doctors and nurses hustled about, talking amongst themselves in quiet tones.

After fifteen minutes of waiting, we were summoned into the room and given this alarming prognosis: The cardiologist had performed an echocardiogram to check Hannah's heart function, and it appeared to be normal. Her decreasing blood pressure might be caused by an infection (hence the fever) which could have been introduced during Hannah's hospital stay or even before. Blood cultures had been drawn to identify the exact infection. Hannah would remain sedated and on the ventilator until she showed signs of improvement.

What happened? Hannah was fine only a few hours ago! We had talked about taking her off the ventilator and now this! An infection—how? We had been so careful to keep Hannah away from others so that she wouldn't get sick before surgery. Were the surgeons not meticulous enough about sterilization to protect her against germs?

Phil and I immediately ran to the computer to inform our prayer warriors about this unexpected complication. Phil wrote:

Our emotions continue to swing. What a wonderful morning it appeared to be, and now we find ourselves wrestling with possible outcomes. Outside of Hannah's room, we simply looked at one another and committed her again into God's hands. He has controlled this from the beginning and is still sovereign over the entire situation. Please continue in prayer. We know that there are so many humbly coming before His throne on Hannah's behalf.

How we depended upon the prayers of our brothers and sisters in Christ! God was indeed sustaining us, giving us enough grace and peace to handle one moment at a time. It seemed as though He was also protecting our hearts and minds from meditating on certain outcomes. As Hannah's health continued to worsen, we hardly considered the possibility of her dying. Sick as she was, we truly didn't believe that death would be the outcome. Hannah was a fighter, proving herself since the age of four months. Surely she would overcome this obstacle, too.

The nurses changed shifts again, and we went back to the waiting room for an hour. At exactly 1:30 p.m., we called into Hannah's room from the hallway phone, asking for permission to come in and see her. They told us that the doctor was placing an arterial line into Hannah's upper thigh, hoping that this might give a more accurate blood pressure reading. It concerned us that we were not allowed back into her room. Didn't they know that we had been waiting patiently for an update for over an hour? No news was good news we were forced to conclude.

At approximately 2:30 p.m., we were permitted to see Hannah and were given an update from the nurse. Hannah's appearance looked disturbing when compared to earlier that morning. She was pale and cool to the touch. There were at least nine different tubes and wires going into her body. The arterial line was giving a more accurate reading, but Hannah's blood pressure had still not stabilized. The doctors administered three different medications to help bring it back up. The fever continued to rise, and she was given another antibiotic which would eliminate ninety-five to ninety-nine percent of all known infections. The effects of the antibiotics would not be seen for a few more hours. All we could do was wait.

We didn't stay long in Hannah's room; it seemed that we were just in the way of the doctors and nurses who were trying to give her the best care. It had been a while since our last posting, so we spent some time on the computer. Whenever we connected to the Website, there were always several messages from our family and friends waiting for us. These were incredibly encouraging during the long hours of waiting. Though physically alone, it felt as though those we loved were right there with us in spirit.

Just as Phil logged off the computer, a nurse we didn't recognize came from behind and touched my shoulder. "Are you Hannah's parents?"

"Yes, we are," I answered, surprised.

"Hannah's blood pressure has suddenly dropped again. There are many doctors and nurses looking after her, giving Hannah medication to raise the pressure up. We will try to keep you informed."

"When can we see her?" Phil asked.

"We'll let you know as soon as she is stable."

"Thank you for finding us," I said in a shaky voice.

Phil's immediate response was to run back to the waiting room where the nurse could easily find us for the next update. I, however, wanted to get back on the computer and update our supporters so that they could pray more specifically for Hannah:

> Nothing so far has been harder to deal with than this. We are not allowed to see her until she is stabilized. A social worker comes out to give us an update whenever she can. I can't bear the thought of bad news, but I know that God is still with us, and His plan is best, whatever most glorifies Him.

Death. For the first time, Hannah's deteriorating health forced me to imagine this outcome. I momentarily contemplated this possibility but refused to take it any further. If I allowed my thoughts to settle on this conclusion, I would have gone insane. There was no use thinking too far ahead—one moment at a time with God's help. *One moment at a time.*

While waiting for more news, Phil and I paced the hallway outside of the waiting room. My thoughts ran wild, fluctuating from life to death and every outcome in between. *Hannah is going to make it,* I reassured myself. *There are so many people praying for her. Surely God is going to see her through this. What a testimony of His faithfulness this will be!* Then, on the heels of this hopeful attitude, ushered in a flood of doubts: *Our daughter is going to die. No, this can't be! Not our daughter. This only happens to other people, not us. How will I ever go on . . . ?*

One moment at a time, Sandy. I continued to mindlessly pace the floor, concentrating on keeping my feet off of the cracks. *Step in the middle . . . Stay off the cracks . . . Step in the middle . . . One foot then the next.* Over and over in my mind I chanted this mantra as a way of keeping myself from thinking about Hannah. Occasionally I sat down on the cold, hard floor and leaned up against the wall to work on my knitting. *Needle through the loop . . . wrap around . . . needle back through . . . slide off.* Between walking and knitting I was able to wait more calmly for an update.

Every time the double doors leading to the Intensive Care Unit swung open, we looked up and held our breath . . . . It was just another parent or staff member, but not our nurse. *What in the world were they smiling about? Wasn't their critically-ill child hanging between life and death like ours?* I resented their happiness and wished there was somewhere to wait more privately. Back to pacing; back to knitting. *When would they come?*

I watched people talk and laugh as they came in and out of the waiting rooms, some of them carrying food that had been purchased from outside the hospital. Several times I had to step out of their way, breaking up my pattern of pacing. Quickly I became irritated with their casualness in this critical setting. This was a hospital not a party!

A group of teenaged girls came around the corner carrying an armful of fast food, and I almost bumped into them. I stepped aside to let them pass and turned back to stare at them in disbelief. "What do they think this is, a *picnic*?" I said loud enough for them to hear. "Have some respect for the hospital!"

Phil could see that the stress of waiting was getting to me. Leaning against the windowsill, he said, "Sandy, calm down. They don't have any idea what we're going through. They're just hungry, that's all. Keep your cool and exemplify Christ, even in our crisis."

I knew Phil was right. How could he be so composed in this situation? I was starting to feel very alone. It was emotionally draining to be told such news and not have anyone except the computer to share it with. No one who saw us could offer any sympathy in our current trial. They didn't know our situation, and it wasn't their fault.

Perhaps the person I was really angry with was God. Why had He chosen us to bear this burden? Did we "deserve" it more than any of these others? I answered my own questions simply, summarizing the truth that He had revealed to me years before: *God is sovereign and in control. Trust Him even when it doesn't make sense.* This was the only consolation that I could give myself, and for the time it was enough. I calmed down and went back to knitting on the floor.

Shortly before 4:30 p.m., a social worker came through the door and made eye contact with us. We knew that she was coming to give us news about Hannah, and, by the expression on her face, it didn't look good.

"Hannah is stable for now," she reported. "She is receiving lots of medication in order to keep her blood pressure up. The antibiotics haven't kicked in yet. We are hoping that when this happens, the rest of her body will also respond."

"Is all of this happening because of the infection?" asked Phil.

"Yes. Hannah's cardiac status is good. It appears that an infection is causing this and not her heart."

"Can we see her soon?" I asked.

"Call back to Hannah's room at four-thirty when the nurses' shift change is over. They will let you know if it is OK to see her then."

"Thank you," we both answered softly.

In the race towards good health we had leaped over one high hurdle but saw many more on the track ahead. In a real competition the hurdles are evenly spaced and expected every so many feet. We didn't have this same assurance. Our hurdles were coming unexpectantly and were set at unpredictable heights. We could only prepare ourselves by being ready to jump at any time, using the strength that God provided to make it over and land safely. I was already out of breath from running, and we had a long way yet to go. How much I relied on God to carry me over each hurdle. Otherwise, without His grace I would have stumbled and fell on the track, unable to get up and move on.

It was another full hour before we were permitted to see Hannah again. There were several nurses and doctors looking after her, more than earlier. I noticed that a crash cart was positioned in the hallway just outside Hannah's room. Yes, this was indeed getting more serious, but just how serious? Were the doctors being totally honest, or were they trying to protect us? I decided that it was time to be bold and ask. I was Hannah's mother, and I had a right to know.

"We've been waiting a long time to get any information," I said to the cardiologist while he stared at Hannah, hand to his mouth as if deep in thought. "Could you please tell us what is happening? We want to know *everything.*"

The cardiologist didn't hesitate to speak with us. Still looking at Hannah, he proceeded to give us the straightforward news that we had waited hours to hear.

"Although the lab results aren't back yet, I'm pretty certain that we are dealing with an infection. By the way Hannah's body is responding, it appears that the infection has entered her bloodstream, and she has gone into septic shock. Because her blood vessels are unable to clamp down and hold in fluids, she cannot maintain enough blood volume which explains why her blood pressure continues to drop. She is currently on four different blood pressure medications and four different antibiotics. If Hannah has another blood pressure episode, there is literally nothing we can do since she has maxed out all of the medications. The next twenty-four to thirty-six hours are critical. Your daughter is one sick little girl."

I wanted to be sure I understood him correctly. What did it mean that she was "one sick little girl?" Since there wasn't anything more that could be done, did this mean she might die? I didn't hear the word "death" in his explanation, so perhaps it really wasn't as bad as it sounded.

"I think I understand what you're saying. On a scale of one to ten, death being ten, how close is Hannah?"

Although he didn't show it, the cardiologist must have thought I was an idiot for asking to put a number on her health status. Didn't I get it? Without pause he quickly shot back: "Hannah is at a nine. She is very close to not making it."

I didn't need to hear another word; I understood now. This was the first time either a doctor or nurse implied that Hannah might die. "OK," I responded, nodding my head up and down several times. I had been told point blank that our daughter was on the brink of death, and surprisingly, I didn't cry or fall apart. That would have been the natural response, I suppose.

It was obvious that God was supernaturally sustaining me in answer to the prayers of our faithful supporters. In my posting to the Website at 5:43 p.m. I gave this update:

We are trying hard to be strong. I don't know what to do with myself. How we depend on your prayers at this moment. Strange as it sounds, we are finding it difficult to pray. This is not because we resent God and His plan for Hannah but because we are stricken with grief.

Pray specifically that her blood pressure will not bottom out again. This has been a waiting game for us. I can hardly breathe sometimes. This has all happened so fast. She looked so good this morning. This is why the doctors suspect it is sepsis. Another episode could happen as fast as the last. We don't know what to expect. Time will tell.

Still trusting the Lord and looking to Him to take care of Hannah whether it's here or in heaven.

Our friends were a little quicker than me to realize the seriousness of our situation. Messages from our prayer warriors began pouring in, messages filled with encouragement and hope from the Scriptures. God had prompted others to console us through His Word, and we drew great strength from reading those verses. God knew that this was the only comfort we needed to get through our crisis *one moment at a time.*

Phil's brother Norm and his wife, Janine, came to visit us later that evening. Shortly thereafter, Joe and Becky Zuzula, two dear friends from church, also arrived to spend time with us. I was so thankful for their company and for the distraction. We all enjoyed a healthy laugh (mostly at Norm's expense), which then prompted a little hunger. Phil and I hadn't thought to eat all day.

The nurses were changing shifts again at 7:30 p.m., so we decided to introduce our friends to the cafeteria. For the past two hours, Hannah had held her own. Her blood pressure had stabilized, and the nurses were slowly weaning her off a few medications. The respirator had been turned up a little because Hannah's lungs couldn't handle the increase in fluids, but overall she seemed to have slightly improved. We left the nurses with our pager number and demanded that they page us if Hannah took a turn for the worse. Her room was only minutes away if we needed to run back from the cafeteria.

Eating food from Wendy's was our only option as the cafeteria was closed. We ordered our meal and sat down to eat in silence. Having been at the table for only a few minutes, our cell phone rang. Phil excused himself to the hallway, answered the call, and found himself talking with a hysterical Moriah.

After being out with the Coreys for most of the day, Moriah had come back to their house and immediately checked the Website to see if we had posted any more messages. Wendy was not expecting there to be any bad news. Last she knew the surgery had been successful and Hannah was doing well. Had Wendy realized what Moriah was about to read, she would have never let her near that computer. Without Phil or I to comfort her, Moriah was a bundle of emotion. She wanted us to come home to be with her, all the while knowing that this was not possible.

While talking with Moriah on the cell phone, Phil's pager went off. It was the Intensive Care Unit calling. Norm, who had followed Phil out into the hallway, ran back to me with the cell phone so that I could continue consoling Moriah. Phil used Norm's phone to call upstairs for an update on Hannah's condition.

The doses of blood pressure medications that had been decreased less than an hour before had to be increased again to the maximum level, as Hannah's body was no longer responding positively to the lower amount. Even though we were still not allowed to see Hannah, Phil wanted to be on the fifth floor so that further updates could be communicated more quickly. I gathered our cold food together by stuffing it into bags and followed Phil up to the waiting room.

The nurses were not ready for us to see Hannah when we arrived, so the six of us sat in the empty waiting room. We talked very little, all wondering the same thing: How was Hannah?

After twenty minutes, Hannah's nurse, Tiffany, came into the room and delivered some disturbing news: Hannah's oxygen saturation level was in the seventies, and her blood pressure had lowered again. Fluid was accumulating in Hannah's abdomen and around one lung. A special doctor had been called to surgically place tubes in her chest and stomach in order to drain the fluid. When the procedure was finished, we could see Hannah again.

Before dinner Hannah seemed to be improving, but now the outlook was completely the opposite. Each time we were given an update, it was progressively worse than the last. It was at this point when I came to accept that Hannah would not live to see her fifth birthday. There was no hope that she would survive. *I have to start facing reality. How else am I going to cope when they tell us she's gone?*

"I just never thought it would come to this," I spoke softly while staring at the floor. "What am I going to tell the kids?"

"She's not gone yet," Becky reminded me. "Take this one step at a time."

I continued to ramble on about the impossibility of this event happening to our family. "She looked so good this morning . . . She was healthy before the hospital . . . She had been doing so well at home." Before surgery I told people that I wasn't worried about Hannah dying—this wasn't an issue of life or death. I was more concerned about helping her through the pain and nursing her back to health. How wrong I was! Our child was dying . . . *our* child . . . *This isn't happening to us . . . This isn't real. Any time now they are going to walk in and tell us that Hannah has made a miraculous recovery. There are so many people praying . . . .*

Another family entered the waiting room and overheard us talking. One of the women, a grandmother, politely asked me to tell her about Hannah. I briefly explained about Hannah's heart surgery and the infection that threatened her life. She listened with a sincere and concerned look, asking me many questions and nodding her head in understanding of my answers.

"I'll be praying for you," the woman encouraged me. She went on to speak more hopeful words, and it didn't take long for me to realize she was also a Christian. She had traveled from Kansas to Michigan with her son and his wife to be a support for her three-month-old grandson. Their baby had his second open heart surgery on the morning of the same day as Hannah's surgery and was recovering well.

Tiffany came back to the waiting room and told us we could see Hannah again for a short time. "She looks pretty bad," she warned us. "Are you sure you want to see her?"

Phil was already out the door. It didn't matter to him how Hannah looked; he just wanted to see his little girl. I was more hesitant. How bad was she? Is this the way I wanted to last remember Hannah? "I think maybe I'll stay here," I answered.

The grandmother from Kansas interjected with some unsolicited yet timely advice: "You should go see her! Whisper in her ear, 'Fight, Hannah! You've got to fight!' By all means, go to her right away! She'll hear you. She needs to know that you want her to fight. That's what she needs to live!"

I decided to see Hannah again, although it wasn't because I thought her life depended on me telling her to fight. I believed that Hannah's recovery depended completely on the will of God. Before the foundation of the world, God planned for Hannah to be born with a defective heart which would then lead to this surgery. February 7 was the day ordained by God for Hannah to waver between life and death. Phil and I trusted our Lord's plan for her life, and with this belief came the solemn understanding that He might choose to glorify Himself more in her death than in her life.

On the Website, Phil considered this truth and wrote the following:

> I'm not sure what more to say. We can only wait and see what God has in store for our daughter. Sandy's and my faith are sure; the Creator of all things has ordained each of our days, including Hannah's. The doctors and nurses are great and trying all they can, but in the end it is God who gives her breath and sustains her. I have no doubt that in life or death, His will is perfect. Oh, how I

pray for life! Sometimes the pain is overwhelming, but He keeps us in His arms.

While difficult, I'll never regret my decision to see Hannah. The nurse had not exaggerated her condition. Hannah's body from head to toe had absolutely no color. Pieces of gauze had been placed in her nostrils to keep her nose from bleeding. More tubes and medications pumped fluids into and out of her frail frame. Another nurse named Rita, continually worked to extract the small amount of drainage from Hannah's chest and abdomen. She explained to us that because of the sepsis, Hannah's blood vessels were unable to constrict and hold fluids. Hannah was "leaking" out into her body, and as a result, the area around her lungs was filling with fluid, making it hard for her to breathe. The chest and stomach tubes drained the accumulating fluid, yet only a little at a time as too much would put a strain on her heart. In order to replace the lost fluids, an equal amount was injected into Hannah's body through an IV, thus maintaining her blood volume and giving the heart enough fluid to continue pumping.

It was easy to see how the delicate balance of fluids in Hannah's body was critical in keeping her from heart failure. Once the antibiotics began to attack the infection then Hannah's condition would improve, and she would be out of the danger zone. We fully understood why the cardiologist said that the next twenty-four to thirty-six hours were the most serious.

I was intrigued with the swift movements of the medical staff and was stunned how all of this effort was necessary to keep Hannah alive. After watching the activity for a few minutes, I snapped out of my stupor and remembered that I was there to visit with my daughter.

I stepped quickly to her bedside, making room for myself among all the machines that covered the floor space at the head of her bed. Tentatively I reached out my hand and placed it on Hannah's brow. Stroking her hair repeatedly, I leaned down and whispered in her ear, "Hello, my love. It's Mama. I'm here with you. Be strong, Baby. Don't leave us yet. Fight this, Hannah. Mama wants you to fight!"

I had told Hannah the very thing that had caused me to be critical of the grandmother from Kansas! In the middle of a crisis, one never knows why certain sentiments are spoken. Perhaps I just wanted her know that Daddy and Mama weren't ready to let her go. Maybe the reminder of her life on earth as part of a loving family would give her the strength to pull through and see us again. In my helplessness, encouraging Hannah was the only thing left for me to do. The rest of it was out of my hands, left to the doctors and nurses who employed their God-given abilities to save our daughter. I've never felt more dependent on other people in all my life.

We only stayed with Hannah for a few minutes. Before leaving I kissed her forehead gently and said, "Good-bye, my angel. I love you."

I did not know that these were the final words I would speak to Hannah. I pray that she heard them. That was the last time I saw her alive. How thankful I am that God intervened, using an intruding stranger to influence me. Without realizing it, this persuasive grandmother was used by God to grant me a final moment to touch and kiss Hannah. Knowing that I was hesitant to see her, He sent another woman to encourage me. It comforts me to know that God cared enough to work out this detail.

After 10 p.m. the updates from the nurses came few and far between. Joe and Becky had to leave in order to relieve their babysitter at home. Norm and Janine hung out with us in the waiting room until around midnight, then left for home to get some needed rest. Since the nurses weren't frequently informing us about Hannah's condition, we assumed she was probably more stable than before. I doubt any of our friends would have gone home if they had thought otherwise. Phil and I remained in the empty waiting room and hallway, trying to keep ourselves from thinking the worst.

Around 1:30 a.m. on February 8, Joe came back to the hospital, this time bringing another close friend with him—Ben Harmon. Phil and I had no intention of going to bed until we heard more news about Hannah, so we were grateful for their company. The four of us sat in the hallway outside the doors of the Intensive Care Unit, conversing about whatever came to mind. Joe and Ben did most of the talking as we could no longer think productively.

A whole hour went by quickly thanks to their efforts at diverting our attention away from Hannah. Finally at 2:30 a.m., one of the cardiologists came to the double doors, opened them slightly, and summoned us to come speak with her. Her facial expression gave away no hint of news, good or bad. My heart pounded through my chest as I held Phil's hand and waited for the update about Hannah.

"How is she?" asked Phil.

The cardiologist didn't mince words. "You had asked earlier how Hannah's brain was reacting to the imbalance of fluid in her body. One of Hannah's pupils is not responding to light. This means that she is bleeding in her brain or pressure is building up in her head. Either one of these is very serious."

"What can be done?" I asked.

"Nothing for the moment. Hannah is too fragile to move downstairs for a CAT scan. She wouldn't survive the ordeal. Unless we know the specific cause, there isn't anything we can do until she stabilizes."

"I don't suppose there is a portable CAT scan machine?" I asked, already knowing the answer.

The cardiologist shook her head. "Unfortunately, no."

"What will this mean for Hannah?" I wanted to know what to expect should we ever make it out of there.

"There are a wide range of outcomes. Hannah could suffer mildly with minimal learning disabilities, or she may never walk and talk again."

This was too much for me to hear. Our options before this news were between life and death. Now the choice of life was tainted with possible retardation and total paralysis. Images flashed through my mind of Hannah drooling in a wheelchair, unable to assist herself or recognize her family. I pictured a life of constant heartache and hardship as we took care of our helpless daughter. Selfishly I didn't want to live this way. *Lord, if this is what will become of Hannah, I'd rather You take her life. Please spare her from a life of meaninglessness.*

Just one hour before I had pleaded with God to sustain Hannah's life, but now I was asking Him to take her home to heaven. I knew that my motives were self-centered and lacked faith.

This was one situation I was sure God couldn't give me enough strength to handle. I had not bargained for this: a life of enslavement to the needs of my daughter. *What kind of mother am I?* I thought. *Where is that unconditional love that I brag about having for my children?*

This was harder news to hear than the possibility of Hannah dying. I didn't want this for me; I didn't want this for her. Hannah would be better off living with Jesus in heaven. Certain that Phil didn't have any of these same thoughts, I refrained from sharing my feelings with him. This was between God and me. When faced with a possible lifetime of suffering, how easily my faith faltered! *O Lord, give me Your strength for I am weak . . . .*

Coming back through the doors, Joe and Ben watched us with worried looks on their faces. We relayed the news to them and sat quietly for a few minutes. Phil and I felt exhausted from the day, and taking in this last update sent us over the edge. Since Hannah's blood pressure had remained stable for the last several hours, we decided to head back to our room and get some sleep. Joe and Ben took this as their cue to leave, realizing that there wasn't anything more they could do except pray and wait. We said good-bye and promised to keep them notified of any changes through the cell phone.

Before going back to the hotel, Phil phoned Hannah's room and let the nurses know where we would be. They assured us that we would be contacted immediately if Hannah's condition worsened or improved.

We stopped off at the computer on our way to the hotel and posted an update for those who were patiently waiting. It had been four-and-a-half hours since our last update. There were countless uplifting and encouraging messages waiting for us to read. It seemed as if no one was getting any sleep that night. Many people were interceding for Hannah on our behalf even if Phil and I weren't. She was covered in prayer, and the outcome was in God's hands.

Once back in our room, Phil put the pager on the nightstand, and we both collapsed on top of the bed covers. We hadn't bothered to turn out the light or to undress. Phil held me close from behind with one arm around my middle. "Good-night," I whispered and was afraid to say anything more. We needed rest, and if I allowed myself to talk about Hannah, tears would certainly spill out and neither of us would sleep. I kept thoughts about possible outcomes to myself, running through them in my tired mind repeatedly. *Hannah is going to die . . . How do you plan a funeral? . . . Brain damage . . . I want the same Hannah back . . . How will I live without her . . . .*

I could hear Phil breathing heavily; he was already asleep. Now it was my turn to rest. If only I could shut off my mind.

Ring, ring, ring! The telephone next to the bed jolted us both awake, and while half-asleep, Phil fumbled for the receiver.

"Hello?" said Phil in a way that greeted the caller and asked—Who is this?—at the same time.

I wanted to believe that the person calling was anyone except a messenger of bad news. I thought to myself, *Maybe it's just Norm calling to get the latest news. My mom hasn't been able to use the computer to get our updates. She might be calling to talk with us. We told the nurses to call us if Hannah suddenly improved. Perhaps her blood pressure was beginning to stabilize, and they are weaning her off the medications.* In just a few seconds I had considered all the possibilities of who might be calling.

My hopes were quickly dashed.

"We'll be right there," spoke Phil to the voice on the other end. My heart sank.

"Hannah has taken a turn for the worse. We need to get down there right away. Put your shoes on fast and let's go."

I jumped to the floor and grabbed for my shoes. While sliding them onto my feet I asked, "What happened? What did they tell you?"

"What I've told you is all that they said. Are you ready?"

I tied my shoes and ran out through the door that Phil held open for me. We ran down the hotel hallway and through the door leading to the hospital. Phil was ahead of me holding doors along the way. The thoughts in my mind kept me from catching up to him. *What has gone wrong? What are they going to tell us? This can't be the end! No, not yet . . . Hannah is strong . . . She's going to make it! There are so many people praying . . . .*

We reached the Intensive Care Unit in thirty seconds. Phil picked up the telephone outside the doors to let them know we had arrived. "What did they say?" I asked Phil, wanting any hint of news before hearing it personally.

Before Phil got the words out, two nurses appeared on the other side of the doors. We walked two steps past the doorway and were stopped in the middle of the hallway. I looked straight into their faces and braced myself.

I don't know who said them, but the next four words changed my life forever.

"Hannah's heart has arrested."

Instantly I burst into tears, my hands covering my face. I knew what this meant. Barring some miracle, Hannah was going to die.

The nurse went on, talking louder over my sobs. "There are many people working on her right now doing all that they can. It doesn't look good."

"No! No! NO!" I shouted, getting more forceful each time. Phil grabbed me from behind and turned me to face him. My knees buckled, and I continued to yell "NO!" while pounding my clenched fists on Phil's body. I wanted to fall down on the floor and throw a tantrum like a two-year-old child. Phil firmly held me up and tried to hug me close. I fought him, yearning to run down the hallway to Hannah's room and beg the doctors not to give up fighting for our daughter's life. I wanted to plead with Hannah to fight and stay with us. No one was letting me do what I wanted, not the nurses or Phil. I was powerless and at the mercy of God's will.

The nurses quickly ushered us across the hall into a cramped room stuffed with furniture. I chose to sit in the rocking chair, and Phil sat in the chair closest to me. Grabbing his arm, I buried my face in the sleeve of his sweater. The nurses asked us to wait until there was more news, and then they let themselves out of the room.

Through the tears, somehow I managed to pray out loud. "Lord, please have mercy on our daughter and save her life. Yet if it is Your will that she go, please help her not to be afraid."

Phil and I continued to cry, both of us stunned and silent. I released the hold on Phil's arm and held my head with the palm of my hand. I closed my eyes and concentrated on breathing deeply, rocking rhythmically in the chair to calm myself down.

In the middle of my random thoughts, suddenly a picture came into my mind. With my eyes still closed, I saw Hannah running. Her head was thrown back, and her long brown hair flowed freely behind. I watched her run a few strides, and then my attention turned to the One she was happily running to meet—Jesus. Hannah was smiling and so was her Savior. She recognized Him and didn't look back once at who was being left behind. There was no hesitation in her step. As Hannah ran closer, Jesus stretched out His arms to welcome her, and she jumped up into His embrace. His arms enfolded her small body and held her tightly, closing His eyes and smiling as if He had just welcomed home a beloved friend after a long absence.

The next vision I had of Hannah was of her dancing. She twirled in circles with arms raised high, laughing wholeheartedly with delight. Hannah's sick body no longer kept her from fully enjoying life. Physical limitations did not hinder her from dancing with the grace of a ballerina. Watching my daughter move in this way made me smile. Hannah was happy, and it pleased me to see her dancing with such joy.

Cutting through the beauty of this image like a knife, I heard in my mind, *Look at your watch.*

I didn't find this thought to be strange or untimely. For some reason I was meant to recall the exact point when I visualized Hannah running to Jesus. I stared at my watch intently, then closed my eyes to remember the time. It was precisely 3:30 in the early morning of February 8.

No more than a minute passed before there was a soft knock at the door. Entering the room were Tiffany and one of the cardiologists who had monitored Hannah's care since yesterday morning. Their sober, downcast faces already told us what they had come to say.

"We have bad news," the cardiologist began. "Hannah's heart arrested. We did everything possible, but we lost her. I am so sorry."

There was a long pause as the cardiologist waited for this news to sink in. As much as we had pondered the possibility of death those last hours, Phil and I were in shock. Nothing could adequately prepare us for losing our child. Even the gradual decline of Hannah's health had not caused us to be more accepting. One never thinks "it" will happen to them. Other people's children die; certainly not ours.

Remembering the vision of Hannah with Jesus, I broke the silence and asked, "What time did she die?"

"Her time of death was pronounced three-thirty."

I nodded my head in affirmation of the vision that God had given me just a minute before. This was the assurance I needed to know that Hannah was safe with Him in heaven. A child that the Lord graciously gave us to raise for four short years had been taken away to an eternal home prepared just for her. An unexpected incident from our perspective, but planned by God before the foundation of the world.

At 4:21 a.m., Phil wrote our concluding update on the Website:

> May the God of heaven, who sees all, knows all, and controls all, give you peace as we write this, our next and final update
>
> Our sweet Hannah is now with the Lord Jesus. It seems hard to believe—just a dream—but God has chosen that she glorify Him in death this day rather than in life. We did not know pain like this was possible. We miss her so much and our hearts ache within us. Please pray for us and see that your faith is not shaken by what appears to be hopeless but is indeed purposeful.
>
> I have no idea what the days ahead will bring. Please be patient with us while we figure this out. The only words that come to mind . . .
>
> God has given and God has taken away. Blessed be the name of the LORD!

It would be another hour before Phil and I were allowed see Hannah. For the time we were calm and contemplative; this was a lot to take in. Thoughts of days to come and memories of Hannah swirled together in our minds. *Phone calls to make . . . her voice . . . a funeral to plan . . . her laugh . . . going home without her.* Once again I focused only on the moment, restraining myself from looking ahead. I needed to save what little strength was left to prepare myself for the next step: holding my daughter's lifeless body and then somehow, letting her go.

5

A Time to Weep

The Sovereign LORD will wipe away
the tears from all faces . . . .

Isaiah 25:8

ALL HUMAN BEINGS, AT ONE TIME OR ANOTHER, HAVE TRIED to imagine what life would be like without a spouse, mother, father, or child. The feelings of despair, sadness, and loneliness are too overwhelming to even think about, let alone live with in reality. Phil and I no longer had to picture the emotions that death would create in our hearts. Our daughter had died, and now we had to face that which we had only imagined. This experience was too real.

The first step in our journey through grief was to make phone calls to the family and friends who had stood with us in prayer during those long hours. We longed for everyone who loved Hannah to be at the hospital with us, sharing in the sorrow of our loss. Only a few minutes had passed since hearing the news, yet already we felt so lonely.

We were thankful the Lord chose to take Hannah home in the middle of the night when no other visitors were around. The hospital did not have a private telephone we could use to phone out. Another alternative was to call people from our cell phone, but we would have to go down to the second floor lobby to use it. Our only option was to use the public telephone in the hallway, located between the two waiting rooms.

It would have been difficult to contact our families in the presence of curious onlookers. We didn't want what was said to be overheard by those who never knew Hannah. Our feelings of pain and grief were very personal and were not meant to draw attention to ourselves. I imagined people passing by and whispering to each other, "I wonder what's wrong with them?"

"I think that their child just died."

"Oh, how sad! Those poor parents."

The Lord, who knew our hearts, spared us from being a spectacle to strangers by sustaining Hannah's life until early in the morning. This was just the first of many ways in which His perfect plan provided comfort to our hurting souls.

We relayed the news to Norm and Janine first and asked them to pass on the information through the church prayer tree. Later Norm told us that the Lord had led him to stay awake and pray for Hannah throughout the night. He knew from our Website updates and phone calls that Hannah's health had worsened since they left us at the hospital. As soon as his telephone rang shortly after 3:30 a.m., Norm knew that Phil was calling with the news of Hannah's death. In the last few minutes of praying for Hannah before she died, the Lord had impressed upon Norm's heart that this would be the outcome, using Psalm 23 to confirm it. Although Norm pleaded with God to save Hannah's life, he knew that God's will would be done for His glory, and he had peace that she would be safe with Christ.

Next Phil called his parents in Florida where they lived during the winter months. Phil's father immediately broke down and sobbed deeply, something that Phil had rarely witnessed him doing. Dad and Mom Dufrin promised to get on an airplane bound for Michigan first thing the following day.

When my father answered the telephone at their home in Clarkston, Phil's words to him were, "Dad, we lost her."

"O God," was his only response. Of all people, my parents would surely know the grief we were feeling. Back in 1968, two years before I was born, my parents lost a daughter, Lisa Ann, at the age of five after a battle with cancer. How the death of Hannah must have brought back a flood of painful memories in their hearts and minds.

Phil then phoned his sister Patti. She agreed to call Phil's younger brother, Doug, who lived in Mom and Dad Dufrin's house while they were in Florida. Then Phil handed the telephone to me.

Although most of our church family had already been informed of Hannah's death, I wanted to personally call my close friend Kristi, with whom I hadn't spoken to since we dropped off the children at her house three nights before.

Both Kristi and I barely said a word as we sobbed together in disbelief. "What will I tell the children?" I asked, not expecting Kristi to answer with advice. "What am I going to do with all of her clothes? How am I going to go on?" My mind was already racing with thoughts of life without our precious Hannah. She had only been gone for twenty minutes, yet I couldn't fathom how we would live the next twenty years.

Following the phone calls, Phil and I went to the computer and posted our last update. Just as we returned to the waiting area, Tiffany came out to tell us that we could go back to Hannah's room. It had been about an hour since her death, and the nurses had finished preparing Hannah by removing the tubes and bathing her body.

We had asked the hospital to refrain from performing an autopsy as it would have delayed seeing Hannah an additional one or two hours. It didn't matter to us that the exact cause of death be determined. This would not have changed our feelings of loss for her or caused us to accept the outcome more peacefully. We had trusted our sovereign Lord from the beginning of Hannah's life and would not waver in our faith now that she was gone.

The room where Hannah had fought for life looked completely different from the last time I had seen it. All the machines had been taken away, and the curtain was drawn to give us privacy. Tiffany went ahead of us and held the curtain back, giving us a view of Hannah's body as it lay in the bed. Phil walked to Hannah's left side first, and I took the other side. The nurses had dressed her in a hospital gown and covered the lower half of her body with "Blankie," a gift sewn by Aunt Janine. Immediately I noticed Hannah's beautiful hair which was pulled back into a ponytail and tied with mauve ribbon.

"Oh, look! They put a ribbon in her hair." The tears flowed freely as I stroked Hannah's head and ran her ponytail through my fingers. Phil was crying uncontrollably, too. We stared at Hannah's body, grappling to understand how her spirit was no longer within but was now communing with the Lord in heaven. She looked so peaceful.

"Do you want to hold her?" asked Tiffany, whose face was stained with tears. "We pulled a large chair next to Hannah's bedside so that you could hold her together."

I walked back around to the other side of her bed and sat in the chair. Phil slid his arms under Hannah's body to pick her up but had trouble lifting her. It surprised us both how stiff and heavy she was. Tiffany assisted Phil from the other side, and together they placed Hannah into my arms.

Tiffany could see that I was physically struggling to hold Hannah comfortably. I wasn't used to the resistance of her arms and legs which did not bend when I tried to move them. She placed two bed pillows under my left arm so that the weight of Hannah's head would not hurt my arms. Though grateful for Tiffany's help, I was still numb and didn't feel much physical discomfort. Even if in the worst pain possible I would have suffered through it for the sake of holding my daughter one last time.

Phil gently lifted Hannah's legs so that he could sit down next to me. "She looks so big laying here in my arms," I said quietly. Hannah's body was stretched out so that her feet dangled over the chair. "Let me see her feet," I said to Phil who then pulled the blanket away and exposed Hannah's petite, size seven feet. I reached my arm across Phil's body and held her foot with my hand, stroking her toes and tickling the bottoms. Only this time, Hannah wasn't laughing as usual.

"She's not here," I said repetitively. "How can that be?" My mind was still having a hard time grasping the separation of the spirit from the body.

I told Phil about the vision God gave me at the time of Hannah's death. "I know Hannah is with Jesus now. She ran to Him, laughing and smiling. Hannah is happy with Christ; why are we so sad?"

Phil and I continued to converse with each other quietly. I picked up Hannah's ponytail and wiped the tears from my eyes with the strands of her hair. "Her hair . . . her hair. Oh, how I will miss her hair."

Not ever wanting to forget her features, I used my middle finger to stroke down the profile of Hannah's face. Starting at her hairline, I dragged my finger down her forehead, between her eyes, to the button-tip of her nose, over the top of her mouth, and then across the lips that I would never kiss again. Over and over I stroked Hannah's face, closing my eyes to sketch her appearance in my mind while speaking softly to her, "I can't believe that you're gone. What am I going to do without you?"

Tiffany peered around the curtain and informed us that visitors had come to see us. Phil summoned them in from the hallway—it was Norm and Janine who had left their home in Williamston the minute after receiving our phone call. The four of us sat together in the dimly-lit room, staring at Hannah's body and crying quietly.

"She looks so big in your arms," said Janine, and I agreed. Perhaps if I had taken the time to cuddle Hannah more it might not have seemed this way. Why wasn't I given more time to spend with my daughter? If only one more day . . . If only one more chance to embrace her on my lap . . . .

A half hour later, a few of my friends from church arrived and were waiting in the hallway. Phil went out to greet them and came back into the room to tell me who they were: Becky, Carmen Harmon, and Helen Lowe. "Helen came, too!" I exclaimed.

Helen's one-month-old son, Dalton, had been hospitalized with RSV at Sparrow Hospital in Lansing. Because of this I assumed she couldn't leave him to make the long trip to Ann Arbor. Then I thought back to a conversation I had with Helen two days before Hannah's surgery. Three separate times the Lord had brought to my mind that I should tell her not to hesitate in coming to the hospital if something bad were to happen. I remembered saying, "I don't know why I'm supposed to tell you this, but if something goes wrong at the hospital (I don't think it will), please come see us. Don't wonder whether you should be there or not—just come."

Helen told me later that if it weren't for me sharing this with her, she would have suspected that I wanted to be alone with Hannah. She would not have left Dalton at the hospital with her husband and drove to Ann Arbor at four o'clock in the morning. I don't know if Carmen would have come to visit us either if Helen had not told her what my wishes were.

It was evident that the Lord had prompted me to give that message to Helen because He knew how much I needed the comfort of my closest friends. Feeling desperately alone, I craved the company of other mothers who could sympathize with the pain of having to give back to God a child that I carried in my womb and nurtured for four years.

Seeing the familiar faces of my friends caused an avalanche of tears to flow. Carmen stepped toward me first and reached down to put one arm around my neck. "Oh, Sandy," she cried as I sobbed without restraint. "I am so sorry." After a long embrace, Carmen let go and Helen stepped forward to hug me. We both cried loudly, neither of us saying a word as the tears spoke volumes. Since I hadn't seen or spoken to them since before Hannah's surgery, their presence during this time greatly soothed my grieving spirit.

Becky and Janine took their turns crying with me also. While still holding Hannah, the five of us talked and touched her body. No one really knew what to say. Over and over I thought about the events of the last hour, and I couldn't hold back any longer. Whether they wanted to hear it or not, I started to tell my friends the story.

I explained how a nurse called us at the hotel just fifteen minutes after we had left the waiting area. I told them what the nurse said as we walked through the doors: "Hannah's heart has arrested." I shared about my tantrum-like response and how I wanted to run down to her room. And lastly I described the vision the Lord gave me just before Hannah died, and how it comforted me. When I finished, everyone was quiet. Focusing my attention back to Hannah, I resumed stroking her hair and caressing her face.

A few minutes of silence passed. My mind continued to replay the final moments with Hannah before and after her death. I couldn't make sense of it. *Our child died. Hannah is never coming back. How can this be true? Please tell me this is just a dream. Dear God, what are you doing? Why Hannah?*

How tempted I was to question the Almighty's plan! Before thinking any further, I made a choice to put my "stake of faith" in the ground.

Looking into my friends' eyes, I broke the silence and declared, "No matter what, I will *not* say, 'This isn't fair!'" They must have thought that the timing of my statement was out of place. Surely I had every reason to rise up against this "injustice." Phil and I were good, loving parents. We had sacrificed much for the sake of our children. Hannah was the happiest four-year-old girl you'd ever meet. Why would the Lord plan this suffering for our lives? Yet who was I to question His sovereign ways? Although my heart had trouble accepting His will, my mind resolved to remain faithful, still trusting that His way was best. We had been given far more than ever deserved! Could I not rejoice and be accepting of both the good and the bad?

Phil asked if he and Norm could come into the room and see Hannah again. My friends decided to leave and wait for me back in the hallway. As they left the room I heard Phil say, "Thanks so much for coming to see us. Sandy really needed you to be here." How true this was. Desperate for someone to share in my sorrows, I cried in the presence of my friends with an intensity that I had not yet experienced. Getting the tears out was indeed refreshing to my soul.

After Norm left, we were alone with Hannah for the last time.

"Would you like to hold her now?" I asked Phil.

"I would like to dance with my daughter one last time."

Phil reached down and took Hannah awkwardly from my arms. The stiffness of her body made Hannah difficult to hold. She didn't cuddle into Phil's chest or wrap her arms around his neck. Her legs didn't squeeze themselves around Phil's waist but dangled down limply instead. There was no life in her body; a living, breathing person was now gone.

I stared at Phil and Hannah in wonder. Her physical body had died, but her spirit still lived on. Our daughter was now with Christ! A small amount of joy awakened in my heart—Hannah made it home! The prayers of salvation for our daughter had been answered. She was where Phil and I wanted her to be, and we would see her again. Even in the midst of sorrow, there *is* hope to be found in Christ.

Each of our five children has a special song that we made up just for them, some put to a familiar tune and others of our own making. "Hannah's Song" perfectly fit her personality: slow, gentle, and flowing. "Hannah Marie-a, sweet Hannah Marie-a, how I love you . . . ." Phil sang the words repeatedly, moving in a circular motion on the floor as I watched with blurry vision through the tears.

After a few turns of dancing, Phil asked me if I wanted to hold Hannah again. I shook my head and embraced the strength from God to let her go. He was helping me to cope with the finality of Hannah's death by giving me the hope of seeing her again in heaven. Apart from the Lord's work in my hurting heart, I would have stayed in that hospital room for days on end.

Phil laid Hannah back down in the bed and covered her with "Blankie." We stood at her side for a few minutes more, just staring at her body and not saying a word. Then, as if we read each other's mind, both of us agreed that it was time to go. I was cried out; there were no more tears. If I didn't leave right at that moment, I might not have had the strength to do so again.

Tiffany followed us out of the room carrying a lavender box tied with a satin ribbon. "Here are some mementos of Hannah for you to take home."

"Is there a lock of her hair?" I asked.

"Yes," answered Tiffany, and she untied the box to show me.

A small lock of hair was tied with thin ribbon and taped to the box. Hannah's name was written below it in purple ink.

"Would you please cut a longer piece of her hair for me?" I wanted this keepsake to always remember how long Hannah's hair was.

Tiffany went right back into Hannah's room and cut a piece of hair just as I requested. She gathered the strands together and tied them with a small piece of ribbon. I held open the box and let Tiffany place the lock into it. "Thank you," I said.

Norm asked to see Hannah one more time. I waited in the hallway with my friends while Phil and Norm went back into Hannah's room to say good-bye. Leaning against the wall in the hallway and fixing my stunned gaze on the tile floor, shock and numbness began to set in. I couldn't think anymore. I didn't have a tear left to cry. There were no words to say. My body was physically tired, but I knew that I could not sleep. Looking to me for clues about how to provide comfort, my silence kept those who surrounded me from uttering a sound. I was certain that my friends were also feeling the shock of this sudden loss as well.

After a few minutes, Phil and Norm left Hannah's room and met us in the hallway. "I guess we'll go back to the hotel room and gather our things now," said Phil.

Yes, that sounded like the next logical step. I didn't know what the following days would hold, but it wasn't necessary to think that far ahead yet. Phil and I had to concern ourselves with getting home to Williamston where we would meet our children and deliver the news.

"Would you like us to help you?" asked Norm. "We can follow you back to the room and help you pack up, if you want."

"Yeah, that would be good," answered Phil.

I could tell that our friends did not want to intrude on this very private moment, yet they had a great desire to assist us in any way. Personally, I wasn't ready for them to leave. Being alone may have caused me to go into further shock. Their company helped to keep me conscious of the events that took place. There was no denying what just happened; this was definitely *not* a dream.

Once back at the hotel room, I sat down on the bed, blocking out the presence of the others while staring at the floor. The memories of spending our last night with Hannah poured into my mind. Only numbness kept me from responding to those thoughts with more crying.

"Sandy, would you like us to pack up your suitcase?" asked Becky.

"Sure," I answered blankly, still looking at the floor.

"Where is your suitcase?"

"In the closet. My clothes are in the dresser."

Phil assisted them by making sure that nothing was missed during the packing. Wanting to be the first person to physically touch Hannah's clothing, I got up from the bed and moved toward the closet like a zombie. I pulled out her floral duffle bag and gently placed it on the bed. The clothes that she wore on the day of her surgery had been hurriedly folded and were sitting on top. I reached into the bag, pulled out Hannah's shirt and brought it to my face.

Breathing in deeply, I desperately tried to catch her scent. I turned the shirt over and over in my hands, searching with my senses to recall what Hannah smelled like. I could detect nothing that reminded me of her. Perhaps Hannah's pajamas would have retained her smell. Unfortunately, no. No matter how deeply I breathed, there wasn't even a hint of Hannah left behind on those clothes. Discouraged, I put them back into the bag and gathered the remaining items from our room: her hair props, the Scoops game, and her winter coat. As I finished, the others had emptied the room of our belongings and were now waiting for us to direct them.

"Can we pray with you before leaving?" Norm asked with great sensitivity. Not knowing what we thought about God during this time, perhaps he didn't want to "push" us to pray if we held any anger or resentment in our hearts. Only by the grace of God did we not harbor any of those feelings. Our understanding of God's sovereignty and the desire to glorify Him in times of joy *and* sorrow, kept us from blaming Him for taking Hannah home earlier than we expected.

Norm led the seven of us in prayer, and while I cannot remember his exact words, I do recall agreeing with them wholeheartedly. Hannah's death glorified God, and He meant it for our good even if I didn't understand how. This is the very definition of faith: believing what one cannot understand. By His great mercy, God had poured out this gift of faith to us from the very beginning. I don't know how else we would have been able to cope.

The walk from our room to the hotel lobby was somber. Our friends carried most of the luggage so that Phil and I could be free to walk together alone. I followed Phil to the reception desk, clutching Hannah's Strawberry Shortcake doll in my hands. We checked out, paid the bill, and began the long walk through the hospital and to the parking structure.

Just outside of the hotel lobby I stopped short and looked down at my empty hands. "The doll—where is my doll?"

I was no longer holding Strawberry Shortcake and couldn't remember where I had set it down. My heart started beating faster as I panicked. Hannah's doll was the last gift I had given her. She adored that doll and hardly put it down. How could I have already lost it?

"Go back and check at the desk," said Phil in a soothing tone. "Maybe you set it down on the counter."

I hastened over to the registration desk and searched frantically across the countertop with my eyes. There, hidden by a fake plant, sat "Strawberry." Breathing a sigh of relief, I called out to the others, "I found her!" They could sense how much I treasured Hannah's beloved doll. Walking away from the desk, I wondered if the Lord had caused me to notice the missing doll. Had I not realized this until we were in the car, I'm sure that we wouldn't have taken the time to go search for it, much to my great loss.

The hospital corridors were still vacant at that early hour of the morning. We walked together in total silence while the others followed behind from quite a distance. Finding our car in the massive parking structure wasn't difficult when compared to previous visits during busier times.

I noticed Hannah's car seat in the back of our small station wagon; this was not the way it was supposed to happen. I had always pictured carrying Hannah out of the hospital wearing the Barbie blanket sleeper that I had purchased just for the occasion. Instead of having light hearts full of joy over Hannah's successful surgery, our hearts were heavy with grief and our arms were empty.

"I don't want to leave you guys!" exclaimed Norm who felt helpless and unsure about leaving us alone.

"We'll be OK," said Phil. "We're going to go home where we will meet the kids and tell them about Hannah. I'm not sure if we'll be in church or not. I guess it depends on how well the children take the news."

"Whatever you decide to do, please let us know. We'll be praying for you."

The car ride home was quiet. I was still in shock. Phil and I didn't talk much about what had happened only three short hours before. Every so often his words would break the silence. I could tell that his mind was more focused on what to do next.

"Where are we going to have the funeral?" he wondered aloud. Our small church of approximately eighty people met at a community center in East Lansing, about twenty miles from our home. The quaint funeral home in Williamston probably wouldn't be able to accommodate the large amount of people expected to attend Hannah's funeral.

"What about First Baptist Church of Okemos?" Phil said. "We have a lot of ties with the people who go to that church. Do you think they would let us have Hannah's funeral there?"

I nodded my head in approval. "That would be nice." While I appreciated Phil's forethought about funeral arrangements, my mind was not ready yet to think through the necessary details.

After another long moment of silence, Phil brought me back to reality with this declaration: "No matter what, let's not let Hannah's death separate us. We need to pray that God will protect our marriage and show us what to do next."

"OK," I quietly answered while reaching for Phil's hand. I don't remember the exact words he spoke, but I do recall Phil's firm tone.

"Let's go to church this morning," Phil suggested at the close of the prayer. "There's no place that I'd rather be than with our brothers and sisters in Christ. What do you think?"

The Lord instantly brought to my mind an event from about ten years before that had made a significant impact on my faith. I was in my early twenties and a relatively new believer in Christ. At the church where Phil and I attended, there was a family whose eighteen-year-old daughter was killed in a car accident while driving home from college. On the morning of her funeral, the father of this young woman stood in the front row at church, praising God unreservedly. His hands were raised up to the heavens, and his voice boomed forth praises to the God in whom he still believed and served. I was blown away by his response. This man had joy even in the midst of this tragedy. I remembered saying at the time, "If that happened to me, I certainly would not have enough faith to stand in church and praise God. O Lord, please give me that kind of trusting faith!"

"Do you remember the Isham family?" was my answer to Phil's question.

"That is exactly what I was thinking, too," said Phil in agreement.

It was decided. The Spirit had prompted us to go and worship the Lord at church among fellow believers. He was worthy of our praise, both for the good and bad circumstances in our lives.

"What about the children?" I asked. "How are we going to get them home from the Calhoun's without raising suspicion that something has gone wrong?"

"I'll call them now and ask if they can bring the kids home at eight-thirty. I want to be the one who tells them about Hannah. I know it will be hard, but Ron and Kristi will have to conceal their grief until our children come back home. Last night Moriah was already concerned that Hannah wasn't doing well. She might be able to read their faces and discern what has happened before we get a chance to tell her ourselves."

"What if the children take it exceptionally hard? Will we still go to church?" I asked.

"Yes, I think so. It will be a good testimony for them to see that God is worthy to be praised no matter what happens."

Phil made the phone call to Ron and Kristi who agreed to innocently mislead the children so that there would be no hint of Hannah's death. Phil and I arrived home at 8 a.m., thereby giving us thirty minutes to unload the car and think through what we would say to the children.

The temperature of our house was freezing; Phil had turned down the heat before leaving for Ann Arbor. I sank down on the living room sofa and kept on my coat. Phil made himself busy by bringing in the luggage and making a phone call to the funeral home. All I had the strength to do was sit motionless on the couch, staring at the walls of the living room. The atmosphere of our home would never be the same. *One less child; one less voice. One less squeal of joy; one less giggle.* The last time I had been home, life felt full. Now I was stripped of everything that was familiar.

The shock that came to me in the hospital still remained. Even as I replayed the last twelve hours in my mind, I didn't cry. There was no denying what had happened, but it seemed as if I was living someone else's life. *This doesn't happen to people like me. They have told us that someone else's child has died, not our Hannah.*

"The kids are here," Phil called out to me as he watched the Calhoun's van pull up the driveway.

I slowly rose from the couch and took off my coat. Walking to the door, I took a deep breath and shuddered, trying to shake the stunned look away from my face. A fake smile came across my lips, and I was sure that the children would not suspect the loss of their sister. I only hoped that they wouldn't look into my eyes. It has been said that the eyes are windows to the soul. My eyes no longer danced with the same joy as they had when life knew no sorrow and all was well.

Phil put on his shoes and helped Ron get the kids out of the van. Greeting them warmly with big hugs and kisses, Phil was also trying hard to be happy. I held the back door open, straining to get a glimpse of the children around our van which was parked in the garage. They looked glad to see us and seemed to have no idea of the news that awaited them.

"Hi guys!" I exclaimed. "Come on in! Boy, did I miss you!"

Moriah and Nathan were the first to come inside. They each took a turn throwing their arms around my waist and holding me tightly.

"Are you surprised to see us?" I asked.

"Mr. Calhoun said that we were coming home to take care of the chickens," answered Moriah. By the tone in her voice I knew that his explanation made sense to her.

"Come in and take your coats off," I said. "Go into the living room and wait for Daddy."

Phil spoke with Ron for a few minutes and then carried Abigail inside. He set her down just inside the door and rolled his eyes. "She's not happy," said Phil flatly with regard to Abigail's disposition.

I reached down to pick her up. "What's wrong, Abigail?" I was used to seeing this sour expression and disagreeable countenance. At the age of two, Abigail was in the prime of exerting her independence. She was known to challenge us at every turn, holding her ground and not breaking easily.

"I want . . . Samantha!" she wailed.

Well, at least two of our children missed us, I thought.

"You'll see Samantha later when we go to church. Aren't you glad to see Mama and Daddy?"

Abigail continued to turn on the waterworks. She was fully sobbing and clearly not glad to be home. I shook my head and sighed. "Go into the living room, Abigail."

Abigail complied but cried loudly the entire way. Phil came through the door and heard the fussing. "What's wrong with her?" he asked.

"She wants to go back to the Calhoun's and play with Samantha."

Phil walked past me and went into the living room where Moriah and Nathan were waiting obediently on the couch. Abigail continued to sob until Phil encouraged her to stop with his firm word. "That's enough, Abigail. You will see Samantha later. Stop crying now and please come sit down."

Phil sat next to Nathan, and I chose the other side next to Moriah. There was no point in delaying. Without discussing it first, both Phil and I instinctively agreed that he would be the one to deliver the news. I was still too much in shock to formulate words. Phil, having more focus than myself, would be able inform the children with equal frankness and gentleness, laying aside his own grief for the moment to help comfort them.

He began slowly and didn't pause between sentences. It was best to come out with it all at one time. "We brought you home early because we have some bad news to tell you. Hannah died early this morning. She became really sick after the surgery, and the doctors tried to make her well, but she just couldn't fight it. Hannah is now with Jesus in heaven, and she won't be coming home."

Moriah grasped it first and immediately began to bawl. I grabbed for her under the arms and brought her to my lap. She covered her face with her hands and cried deep, body-wracking sobs. Though it seemed I had no more tears to cry, my eyes began to fill again, and I joined Moriah's lament with soft crying of my own. Her heart was hurting too, although only a fraction of my pain as Hannah's mother. Yet even that small part was too much for an eight year old to handle. How I wanted to take the hurt away!

While comforting Moriah I glanced over at Nathan who sat quietly without moving a muscle. By the expression on his face I could tell that he was still processing the news he just heard.

"Son," said Phil tenderly, "do you understand what I just said?" Phil's tone was gentle and soothing though the words themselves were harsh. "Hannah's gone and we will never see her again here on earth."

Nathan's lip began to tremble, and a single tear started flowing over his round red cheek. He remained silent, staring straight ahead and dealing with the pain of losing his sister in his own way. We didn't reach out to console him, for that would not have been what he wanted. Nathan needed a moment to sort out his feelings and to process this unexpected news. I continued to observe his face, looking for an indication that he needed a loving embrace from his dad or mom. As Nathan tried to make sense of Hannah's death, the tears began to flow, and Phil pulled him closer to provide comfort.

Abigail had quieted down long enough to hear Phil tell the others about Hannah, but the news didn't seem to phase her. How much of what we said could a two year old comprehend? Seconds later, Abigail's self-centeredness was in full force again as she worked herself into tears over having to leave Samantha.

"Abigail, come here, Honey," I said. She reluctantly walked over the couch where I was still holding Moriah. Looking right into her face I asked, "Did you hear what Daddy said about Hannah? She got real sick and died last night. Now she will live with Jesus in heaven instead of with us. Do you understand?"

Abigail didn't respond in word or action. She pulled away from me and began prancing in the middle of the living room floor. Helping her to realize our loss was going to be tougher than I anticipated.

"Abigail, where is Hannah?" I called out to her, searching for some evidence that she had heard me.

Without breaking the step of her dance, she answered, "Living in heaven with Jesus." Abigail was just repeating what I told her moments before, but I was glad that she had listened!

I continued to comfort Moriah who was having a hard time getting her emotions under control. "I'm so sorry that the two of you have to go through this at your age," said Phil. Looking at me but still speaking to them, he said, "It doesn't seem right that a kid must experience so much grief."

I continued Phil's line of thought. "We had no idea that this would happen to Hannah. The doctors told us that she would recover from the surgery just fine. But that wasn't God's plan. Before Hannah was even born, God had chosen that this would be the day when she would go home to be with Him."

"We have taught you that God is always in control," said Phil. "Hannah's death does not surprise Him. We have also taught you that being a Christian doesn't mean life will always turn out the way we want it. So no matter what happens, good or bad, we will still continue to trust in the Lord even if it doesn't make sense to us."

This was a lot for a child to comprehend, but it wasn't the first time they had heard us say it. We made certain to instruct our children that being a Christian didn't guarantee a rosy life. Trials and suffering are hardships that God uses to build our trust and faith in Him. Following Christ means we are to surrender our own will and submit ourselves to His plan for our lives, in both times of joy and suffering. These truths from Scripture were not foreign to our children.

Phil waited through a few minutes of quiet before continuing. "Today is Sunday. Mom and I have decided that we will go to church, just like always. In spite of our grief, God is still worthy of our praise. We want to go and worship the one true God who has made a way through Christ for us to see Hannah again. Is that OK with you?"

Both of them answered with an approving nod. "Do you have any questions about what happened?" I asked. "You can ask Dad and I anything."

Neither Moriah or Nathan responded. I wish that I could have read their minds! What *were* they thinking? Were they angry with God or accepting of His plan? Did they fully understand the finality of Hannah's death? Perhaps their quietness was only a result of the shock they felt in just hearing that they would never see their sister again on this side of heaven. I didn't want to push them into talking about it before they were ready, but I also wanted them to know that the door was always open to share their feelings.

"Let's get ready to go then," said Phil.

Abigail was still flouncing around the living room. "Abigail," I called out to her, "where's Hannah?" I was curious about her response, wondering if it had changed from before.

"She's living in heaven with Jesus."

"Why is she with Jesus?" Her reply might tell me more about how much she remembered our conversation.

"Because she died."

"That's right, Abigail. Hannah is with Jesus now, and He is taking good care of her."

I knew that Abigail did not really understand death, but she certainly exhibited the childlike faith to believe that Hannah was living happily with Jesus in heaven. Not once did she question our explanation or ask us, "Where's Hannah?" I had expected that Abigail would need repeated reminders of where Hannah had gone. On the contrary, it was *I* who continually asked Abigail to tell *me* where Hannah was!

The twenty-minute ride to church was quiet, but thoughts of the last twenty-four hours screamed inside my head. I couldn't shut off the noise. I forced myself to look ahead but only so far as the worship service at church. *One step at a time.* Right now God wanted me to trust Him for the next step and nothing more. The grace to endure the following days, weeks, and months would be there as I needed it and not a moment too late.

As we pulled into the parking lot, Helen's husband, Matt, spotted our van while driving home from the hospital where Dalton was being treated. He followed us into the parking lot and greeted us with silent tears and a big six-foot hug. I had hoped that Matt and Helen would be able to worship with us at church, but Dalton had not been discharged from the hospital yet. Apparently it was not part of God's plan for them to be with us that Sunday, and, although I was disappointed, it was one more opportunity to place my trust in God.

The Dufrin children had never been known to walk casually though the large, wooden doors of the Hannah Community Center where we met for church. Usually Moriah or Nathan ran ahead to hold the door for Hannah and Abigail to scurry through, followed by Phil and me from several yards behind. Once inside, the kids always stopped at the front desk to converse with Ed, the receptionist, who was always genuinely glad to see us.

The same was true of that morning, minus one child. Moriah and Nathan raced ahead to hold open the door for Abigail who passed through without Hannah giggling by her side. Phil and I brought up the rear, both feeling the pain of observing life without Hannah. This was just the first of many typical life experiences when we had to do something for the first time without Hannah's presence. Would it always hurt so much?

Many people had already gathered when we arrived on the second floor. Before entering the sanctuary, I was surrounded by my fellow sisters in Christ who embraced me hard and long, sobbing without saying a word. Carmen had scooped up Moriah who was crying loudly just as she had at home with me. I can't recall another time when Moriah was so vulnerable in the company of another adult. I was thankful that she allowed Carmen to comfort, pray, and minister to her while I focused on my own grief.

I was received by my friends with such overwhelming love and support. What a picture of how the body of Christ is supposed to function! All disagreements on doctrine and conviction had melted away. Christ became central as people pulled together to bring us comfort and encouragement. Our church, though small in number, has never been small in their devotion to Christ and one another as was evidenced on that day.

Through the years, Phil and I have been frustrated by the lack of numerical growth within Covenant Life Community Church. People commit themselves for a time then leave, some with good reason and others for no apparent reason. God had chosen to keep our church small, like that of a family unit where everyone knows one another intimately. There had been moments when I wanted to hide myself within a large congregation so that no one else would know my business! But after losing Hannah, I was so grateful for the fellowship we shared together as fellow brothers and sisters. Romans 12:15 says, *"Rejoice with those who rejoice; mourn with those who mourn."* Every person in our church body was touched and affected by Hannah's death. For many of our friends, Hannah was loved like one of their own children. There is no other church I want to be part of, unless God moves us into ministry of our own.

Norm decided to keep the service short so that we could spend more time together, fellowshipping in our grief and rejoicing that Hannah had gone to heaven. We gathered to worship through song for about twenty minutes. Aside from the day of our wedding, this was one of the most meaningful times of worship I had ever experienced. Every song seemed to relate to our situation, and the words we sang out to God could not have been more glorifying to Him!

Two selections that stick out most in my memory were: "The Wonderful Cross" and "Be Unto Your Name." Because of their relevancy to our trial, I've included the words to the second song below. That morning I found these words to be extremely comforting to my soul, and God used them for weeks after her death to console me.

We are a moment, You are forever.
Lord of the ages, God before time.
We are a vapor, You are eternal;
Love everlasting, reigning on high.

Chorus:
Holy, holy, Lord God Almighty,
Worthy is the Lamb who was slain.
Highest praises, honor and glory
Be unto Your name. Be unto Your name.

We are the broken, You are the healer.
Jesus, Redeemer, mighty to save.
You are the love song we'll sing forever,
Bowing before You, blessing your name.

As I sang out to God, tears of sorrow and joy flowed down my face. I couldn't imagine my life without Hannah, and, until the Lord calls me home, I would not see her again while on earth. Yet mixed with these bitter tears were cries of joy. Because of Christ and His death on the cross to pay for my sins, I *will* see Hannah again! What hope I have! This life isn't all there is to offer. For those who love Christ, heaven waits for us beyond the hardships and trials we presently suffer. Hannah made it there. She has seen the

God of all creation! She sits before the throne of our living God, worshipping Him for all eternity.

Following the service, I walked directly over to Kristi whom I had spoken with on the phone but had not yet seen. I longed for consolation from my friend who loved Hannah so much.

I wished that Kristi could have been at the hospital to see Hannah one last time. I had given her the responsibility to care for my children and asked her to stay with them through the night in case one of them awoke unexpectedly. If Nathan or Moriah (who spent the night at the Calhoun's) woke up and needed Kristi, they would surely know something went wrong if she wasn't there. I was adamant about the children hearing the news of Hannah's death from Phil and I. So to protect them I asked Kristi to stay home instead of coming to the hospital.

Later Kristi assured me that she was glad the last remembrance of Hannah was of her alive. Two weeks prior to Hannah's death, Kristi cared for my children overnight in her home so that we could meet with the heart surgeon in Ann Arbor. Before waking Hannah in the morning, Kristi felt compelled to pause and stare at her peaceful sleeping form for several minutes. This was one of Kristi's last memories of Hannah. She was satisfied that God must not have wanted her to see Hannah's lifeless body laying in my arms. Maybe it would have been too much for her to handle.

Several of the other ladies soon joined us, and they encircled me to pray. Moriah stood right by my side the entire time. After praying, I stayed to talk with those who had gathered, relaying the events of the last two days. Everyone listened patiently and asked questions along the way. It was a time that helped me to sort out what had just happened. Perhaps the noise in my head would be quiet for a little while.

The Coreys and Harmons asked if they could bring pizza back to our house and visit with our family. I didn't want to be alone in the house where just four days before we lived and laughed together as a family of seven. The company of others would provide a distraction, delaying the experiences of ordinary living for a time. I wasn't ready to go back to life as normal: making lunch for the kids, putting them down for naps, and taking a Sunday nap myself.

The adults sat together in the living room while the kids played in the basement. I truly did not care what they were doing or where they were—that was definitely not normal for me! Carmen took over as mother to the children, supervising their activity and meeting their needs.

At three o'clock in the afternoon Patti returned Samuel to us. I was glad that he was home, but I didn't have the physical or emotional energy to care for him. Patti sensed this and offered to stay and help out, which I agreed to immediately. Shortly after Samuel's arrival, the Calhoun family came over to join us. We sat together at the kitchen table and made light conversation, none of which was directly about Hannah though she was constantly on everyone's mind.

Phil spoke with the funeral home in Williamston again, and the director asked us to meet with him at ten o'clock on Monday morning to make the arrangements. He also told Phil that we should bring an outfit for Hannah to be buried in.

"I'll have to run out and buy a dress for her," I said.

"Isn't there anything in her closet that she can wear?" asked Phil.

"Not really. All of her church dresses are too casual. Would you mind if I went shopping for her right now? I really want to find something special."

"Honey, you do whatever you want. You're better at this kind of thing than I am."

I was so pleased that Phil gave me the freedom to shop for Hannah. It brought a small bit of joy to my heart knowing that I had one more opportunity to choose something special for my daughter. It was like hunting for the perfect wedding dress.

I asked Kristi to come along with me, and, just as I expected, she was the perfect shopping partner. We were short on time—it was Sunday and the stores closed at 5 p.m. This only gave us an hour to make a selection. Moriah and Emily, Kristi's daughter, begged us to let them come also. Allowing the girls to tag along might have slowed us down some, but how could I deny my oldest daughter the experience?

We both agreed that our best chance of finding a suitable dress was at The Hickory Limb, a children's specialty shop. Since it was February, many of the winter dresses were already on clearance in order to make way for Easter dresses. The saleswoman directed us to the sale rack, but I didn't see anything that spoke "Hannah" to me.

Returning to the front of the store, I spied a solitary rack which held one style of dress in various sizes. It was cream in color and was covered in mauve, pink, and light green roses. The short sleeves were elaborately decorated with satin rosettes that matched those on the waistline. I pulled the dress off the rack and held it up for Kristi to see. "What about this one?" I asked.

"I actually saw that dress right when we walked in the store. It reminds me a lot of Hannah. Do you like it?"

"The fabric, style, and color are perfect, but it has short sleeves." Hannah had many needle pokes in the hospital, and I didn't want those to show.

"Maybe they also have a cardigan sweater that would go with it," suggested Kristi. "I'll go ask."

The saleswoman took Kristi to the back of the store and pulled out several sweaters to choose from. One in particular matched the best, but I wasn't satisfied with the color.

"I was hoping you had a mauve sweater to match the flowers in the dress. Do you think that the mall might have one?" I asked.

"You aren't likely to find just the right color of pink, but you never know," said the saleswoman. "Do you need to have this tonight? Who are you shopping for?"

I swallowed hard. This was the first time I had to tell someone that my daughter had died. How should I say it?

"My four-year-old daughter died early this morning. I have to find her a dress to be buried in by tomorrow morning."

"Oh, I'm sorry," responded the woman. In spite of the late hour, she was a lot more patient and helpful with us than before.

I decided it was worth a quick look at the mall across the street to see if there was another sweater that would match. I dragged Kristi with me from store to store but turned up nothing.

As I passed by the other shoppers and looked into their faces, I thought, *My daughter died today and none of these people I'm passing by have a clue as to the pain I feel.* From this experience I learned to use caution when making snap judgments about the people I meet. No one knows from just one glance the hardships that others have faced. I ought to give more grace to those who act rude or foul; perhaps they are going through a difficult time and are just letting the pain show through.

The time was now 4:50 p.m., and The Hickory Limb would be closing in ten minutes. Kristi called the store from her cell phone as we ran back to the car. They agreed to remain open for as long as we needed. I finally resolved that the dress and cream sweater were perfect for Hannah; the style was truly "her." Why hadn't I realized it before? Like a true woman I needed to see all my options first before deciding this dress was "the one."

I also purchased matching dresses for Moriah and Abigail off the clearance rack. They were plum velvet on the top with a floral print on the bottom. Not really either Moriah or Abigail's color, but the style was right for the occasion.

On my way to the counter to pay for the dresses, I saw a dainty pearl bracelet that had a tiny silver cross dangling from it. It was the perfect compliment to Hannah's dress and sweater, and I added it to my purchases.

"I'd like to pay for Hannah's dress, if you don't mind," offered Kristi.

"Certainly I mind! This dress is expensive! You don't have to do that."

"No, I want to. Please, let me buy this for Hannah."

I sensed Kristi's need to contribute in some way. And since she was known as Hannah's "Second Mother," I understood her desire to pay for the dress.

Next we drove to the craft store to choose a ribbon for Hannah's hair. From there we shopped for tights and then headed to the shoe store. Hannah's feet would not be seen in the casket, but *I* knew her outfit would not be complete without a matching pair of shoes.

Ron called Kristi several times from our house, gently pleading with us to come home soon as my parents had arrived and were anxious to see me. We finished the last of our errands and raced home.

Once back at the house, we found Ron and Patti in the kitchen cooking spaghetti for dinner. Phil was upstairs sleeping—it had been a long day. All of the children were playing in the basement.

I proudly displayed the dresses for Hannah and the girls to my mom and Patti. The dress shopping experience put me in a great mood. The bantering between Ron, Patti, and my mom also helped to keep things light. No one talked about Hannah, but I knew she was on everyone's mind.

When dinner was ready, I was served first at the table. Having no appetite, I ate very little. The time was now 7:30 p.m., and the exhaustion of being awake for almost thirty-six hours was finally catching up with me. I could have fallen asleep right there in the chair.

My mom and dad left shortly after dinner, and Kristi encouraged me to head up to bed for the night. "We'll clean up and put the kids to bed. Don't worry about anything. You need some rest."

I didn't argue. Sleeping sounded good, and I was tired enough to fall asleep without the events of the day giving me insomnia.

While getting ready for bed, Phil woke up and asked me how the shopping went, who was still at our house, and where the kids were.

"Patti and Kristi are taking care of everything downstairs," I answered. "We found the perfect dress for Hannah. I'm sure you'll agree when you see it tomorrow."

Before getting into bed I went over to Hannah's suitcase which was sitting on the floor in my bedroom among a heap of other bags. Hannah's nightgown was laying near the top. I pulled it from the bag and held it up to my face. Breathing in deeply, I tried to catch a scent of her but smelled nothing but fabric.

I took the nightgown with me to bed and slept with it tucked under my arms near my chest. Phil and I talked for a few minutes more, recalling the past few days. I had felt strong and encouraged all throughout the day, but now, with no distraction from others, I began to cry. I already missed Hannah so much. Phil snuggled up close to me to provide comfort.

"I know, Honey. I miss her too," he whispered.

After an hour had passed I fell asleep in the midst of crying. Would the first night without her be the hardest, or would it get easier as time went on? I could never imagine my grief ever feeling easy.

We made it through the first day of living without Hannah. God's grace was there to help us, just as He promises. The next day had a whole new set of emotions tied to it, but again God would help us to bear it . . . *one step at a time.*

God's most beautiful thoughts bloom into children. Our new "blossom," Hannah Marie, was born on August 2, 1999.

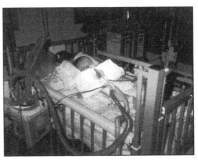

Four-month-old Hannah contracted RSV in December of 1999 and almost lost her life. By God's grace she was allowed to live. After 23 days, Hannah came home and finished her recovery while in our care.

Dressed up for a wedding in March 2000. Hannah is seven months old, Nathan is two years old and Moriah is four.

While camping in late May 2000, Hannah wore this "babushka" to keep her warm. (Mama had forgotten to pack her a hat!) Shortly after this, Hannah was hospitalized for twenty-six days with pneumonia.

Sandy with eleven-month-old Hannah in June 2000 during her second long hospitalization.

Sandy holds Hannah in their back yard just before Hannah's first birthday in July 2000.

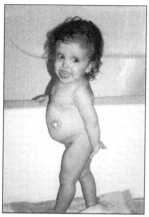

"Mama, you're embarrassing me!"
Hannah models the gastronomy tube that
helped her to fatten up and gain strength.

Here comes trouble! Hannah became locomotive by
scooting on her bottom. Nothing on the floor was safe
anymore. (January 2001, 17 months)

Hannah, our summer beauty, in June 2002 at 22 months.

Phil and Hannah at the Toledo Zoo where our family took a
mini-vacation during the summer of 2002.

At the age of two, Hannah slept for the first time in
her "Big Girl" bed.

Hannah holds her favorite book, *Jesus Loves Me,* a gift
given by Phil for Valentine's Day in 2003.

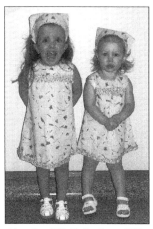

Hannah and "Bobby" at Easter 2003.

"No matter what happens, I will always love you."

Hannah and Abigail were always together and dressed alike quite often. This picture was taken while camping in August 2003. Hannah had just turned four and Abigail was two.

A painting project as part of our homeschool curriculum.

Playing dolls was one of Hannah and Abigail's most enjoyable activities. In this picture they "nurse" their babies, just like Mama!

Dueling potties! Abigail finally "pushed" Hannah to potty train at the age of four in October 2003.

Hannah loved doing "school" with her siblings. This is one of
Sandy's favorite pictures of Hannah, taken in September 2003.

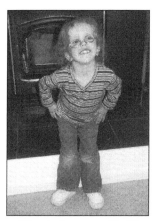

"Hannah, give me some 'hips'!"

Groovy girl!

"Catch me if you can!"

Phil colors with Hannah at our kitchen table, an activity they
enjoyed doing together often. Hannah pretends to wear a
veil on her head made from a blanket.

The Dufrin cousins at Christmas 2003. Back row from L to R: Tory, C.J., Brennan, Moriah, Colette, Ian, and Nathan. Front row from L to R: Hannah (the only one not looking at the camera), Abigail, and Maddie. Samuel and Doug are not pictured.

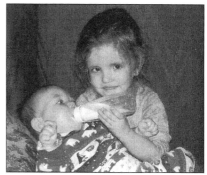

Hannah, age 4, feeds seven-month-old Samuel in January 2004.

January 2004. Nathan (6), Abigail (2), Hannah (4), Moriah (8), and Samuel (8 months)

Ponytail Pals! This picture was taken at the Calhoun's house two weeks before Hannah died. From L to R: Emily, Hannah, Samantha, Abigail, and Moriah.

Our family photograph, taken in our living room exactly one week before Hannah died. At the time, none of us imagined it would be the last picture taken of the seven of us together. Today, a 16 x 20 copy printed on canvas hangs above our fireplace.

The last photo of Hannah and her siblings, taken two nights before her surgery on February 4, 2004. Samuel, who had gone to Aunt Patti's house earlier that day, missed out on the picture.

Hannah snuggles into her bed at the Med Inn on the night before surgery. She is wearing the purple princess nightgown and holds her Strawberry Shortcake doll, both gifts from our family.

"Where's the blue truck, Hannah?" "I see it, Daddy!" Phil and Hannah keep themselves entertained in our hotel room on the morning before her surgery.

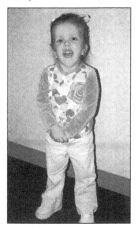

The last picture of Hannah alive, taken from our hotel room just before walking to the surgical waiting area on February 6, 2004.

Our family enjoys cider and donuts near Hannah's grave site on a warm fall day in October 2004. Sandy is seven months pregnant with Baby Dufrin and due in early December.

Almost one year after Hannah's death in January 2005, the Dufrin children pose for the traditional "New Baby Line-Up." A space is made in the middle where Hannah would have been. Aaron Peter Dufrin, the last of our six children, is five weeks old.

6
Wedding Plans

Let us rejoice and be glad and give him
the glory! For the wedding of the Lamb has
come, and his bride has made herself ready.

Revelation 19:7

IT ONLY TOOK THREE SECONDS AFTER OPENING MY EYES FOR that sinking feeling of great loss to tie a knot in my stomach. *Hannah has died. She is never coming home, and I will never see her again until God takes me to be with her. How will I possibly get through this day?*

I had slept soundly through the night and felt rested but had no desire to get out of bed yet. Phil was already awake laying next to me. I rolled over and forced a smile. "Have you been awake for long?"

"Yeah, I woke up early and couldn't get back to sleep. I've just been laying here, thinking."

There was no point in asking what was on his mind. Neither of us could think of anything other than Hannah. "What time is it?" I asked.

"A little after seven. Samuel is just starting to stir. Do you want me to bring him to you before his crying wakes up the others?"

"Sure. I'd appreciate that."

A minute later Phil and Samuel appeared in the doorway of our bedroom. Phil carried him into the bathroom to change his diaper before handing him off to me to nurse.

"While you feed him I'm going to take a shower," said Phil.

"Go ahead, and take your time. I'll just be here with Samuel."

Oblivious to my grief, Samuel nursed contentedly. Nothing in his little world was any different than before. I knew that he would never remember his sister, and for Samuel's sake this saddened me. Hannah loved and adored him so much! It was Hannah who gave Samuel his first nickname—"Sambla"—because she couldn't pronounce his name properly. It was Hannah who called him her "Little Man." Samuel may not be able to recall any memories of living with his sister, but we would certainly see to it that he knew who Hannah was and how much she cherished him.

Phil and I spent the rest of the morning preparing to leave for the day in order to make funeral arrangements and do some shopping. Patti and her three children arrived at 9:30 to help out around the house, hosting the guests who stopped by and answering the telephone.

Our meeting with the funeral home director was scheduled for 10 a.m. We asked Norm to come along so that he could take note of the details that our church would need to assist with. The three of us sat down with Mike, the director, and discussed the particulars of Hannah's visitation, memorial service, and burial.

Neither Phil nor I had ever been responsible for planning a funeral. Mike spent a lot of time gently educating us on what to expect over the following three days. I was impressed that the funeral home took care of practically everything. What they could not provide, such as the meal following the service, was handled by our church. Phil and I did not have to worry about a thing. Missing Hannah took enough of our physical and emotional energy. The stress of planning a funeral in addition to our grief would have been too much to handle.

Discussing Hannah's funeral arrangements did not seem real. Instead of deciding on flowers for our daughter's wedding, we were choosing flowers to adorn her casket. Everything we selected—the flowers, funeral program, and casket—had Hannah's sweet temperament in mind. The bright yellow and orange flower arrangements did not have a hint of anything that looked sad or "funeral-ish." A fuchsia daisy pictured on the cover of the program had the following sentiment written underneath: "The memory of her love is as beautiful as a flower forever blooming in the garden of our lives." The casket we chose was simple in design and was covered with soft white fabric.

I asked if we could place pink rose petals around Hannah's body so that it appeared as if she were lying on a bed of flowers. Although unusual, Mike expressed that this was a thoughtful idea and didn't foresee any problem arranging it. I also inquired about placing a small Bible in Hannah's hands. Liking this suggestion as well, Mike told us to bring the Bible before the visitation so that we could place it in her hands ourselves.

The same feeling I had as we shopped for Hannah's burial dress came over me as we agreed on plans for the funeral. This was the closest thing to planning the wedding that she would never have. It was my final opportunity to take care of Hannah's needs and was the last physical act of love that I could show my daughter.

The visitation was scheduled for Wednesday afternoon and evening. The funeral home could not accommodate us until that time due to another funeral. Now we had all of Tuesday to rest before the memorial service which was set for Thursday at 1 p.m. at First Baptist Church in Okemos. The gracious people at First Baptist were more than willing to assist us by taking care of the music, sound, and custodial services.

Following our meeting at the funeral home, Phil and I stopped home to take Nathan's measurements for a suit. Patti had everything under control, and Samuel was doing well without me, so we headed off again to meet the curator of Summit Cemetery in Williamston.

We had been told that this cemetery, just four miles from our house, was one of the nicest in the county. Although covered with a thick blanket of snow, we agreed with this assessment from the moment we drove between the thick, brick pillars which lined the road front. I had driven past Summit Cemetery numerous times before but never stopped to notice the breadth of land it covered or the beauty within.

In the old section, monuments filled every space. The etchings on the marble stones were worn away by the elements of time and weather. The new section was adorned with hardy granite monuments, dating from the 1980's until present. Large trees, both deciduous and evergreen, were interspersed among the grave markers, providing shade and mature magnificence. It appeared that the cemetery grounds were neat and well cared for. This was the perfect final resting place for Hannah's body.

The man we were scheduled to meet with—Ben—was already waiting for us. He was a short, elderly gentleman who had a strong physical stature. Ben's assistant, Mark, was a younger fellow who was being trained to take over Ben's position whenever he decided to retire.

Mark welcomed us and introduced Ben. "He knows by name where every person in this cemetery is buried. Ben's worked here for most of his life. He used to dig the graves by hand until just recently when we got this backhoe to do the job."

Phil held out his hand to Ben. "Nice to meet you, although not under these circumstances, of course."

"Sorry to hear about your daughter," said Ben, who only paused a moment before getting right down to business. "You'd probably want to pick a site that is in either this section or this section," he said, pointing to the south and southwest sections, respectively. "That's where the new grave sites are located. Everything to the right of us is the old section."

Phil and I liked the south section best, and we inquired about the available plots in this area. Ben pulled out a large book filled with plot maps and names.

"We have plots available over there," he said, showing us the master book. "You can basically pick wherever you want."

"My wife and I would like to purchase three plots, one for our daughter and two for us. Can you show us what the options are?"

"Let's walk over and take a look at the land. You might get a better idea of what you want by seeing it firsthand, instead of on paper."

The four of us stood on the road alongside the south section. The wide-open area was closed in by a fence lined with evergreen trees on the opposite side. "What about a plot under a tree? Are there any left?" Phil inquired.

"I wouldn't recommend that," answered Ben. "The sap from the trees makes an awful mess on the grave markers."

Phil and I quietly looked over the area for a few minutes. Since we had no other family buried there, our choices were fairly unlimited. We decided to choose three plots directly in the middle of the open space. There were no other graves near these plots, at least for now. We liked the idea of having the entire field to ourselves with a place for Hannah's siblings to run and play without disrespecting those who were buried there.

Ben informed us of the preparations that would be required before the funeral. The grave site would be dug on Tuesday and the tent placed over it on Wednesday morning. The snow would be cleared away so that access to the grave was not hindered. The township office would send us the bill for services a few weeks following the funeral. There was nothing else for Phil and I to concern ourselves with at the cemetery.

Before leaving, our conversation turned to other "trivial" matters. Mark talked about his family and an upcoming trip to the Bahamas with his wife. Ben remained quiet except when Mark mentioned taking an airplane to get there. "You won't ever get me on an airplane!" he exclaimed. "Those things are death traps!"

"Well, you know, Ben," I answered. "When it's your time to go, God will take you whether in an airplane or not."

"That may be," Ben replied, "but you still won't get me into one of those things. They're dangerous."

Hannah's recent arrival into heaven certainly caused me to look at life differently and to be more bold about the destination of other people's souls. Before Hannah's death I would have never made a comment like that to someone whom I'd just met!

It may have seemed inconsiderate of Mark to ramble on about the details of his vacation to people who had just lost their daughter. But I truly wasn't bothered by this. Mark and Ben worked in a cemetery where they spent the majority of their daytime hours surrounded by the dead. They may have been extremely comfortable with the topic, forgetting its newness to us. Or perhaps because they did not know Hannah personally, her death did not phase them. As caring and kind as they were, to them, Hannah was just another body to dig a grave for.

The meeting at the cemetery took about an hour overall. Phil and I called home to check on the children before driving out to the mall in Okemos. Both Phil and Nathan needed a suit, and I wanted to look for a dress to wear at the visitation or the funeral. Two months before in December, Phil had purchased a black dress for me to wear to a wedding. Not certain about what else was in my closet, I wanted to find another appropriate outfit just in case nothing else fit me at home.

Our next stop was across the street at the Christian bookstore. We needed to purchase a Bible for Hannah and choose the music to be sung at the funeral. The popular funeral song of that time was "I Can Only Imagine" by Mercy Me. While I thought this song was appropriate for Hannah's funeral, I was intent on finding something more specific to the death of a child.

The clerk at the store saw me searching through the hundreds of song titles and came over to offer her assistance. "What occasion do you need the song for?" she innocently asked.

I wasn't sure how to formulate the words without breaking down into sobs. "Well," I began, forcing a smile, "our four-year-old daughter died yesterday morning. Her funeral is scheduled for Wednesday, and we need a song for the soloist to sing in memory of her."

"Oh, I'm . . . sorry," stammered the woman. She was visibly shocked and didn't know how to respond. I waited for her to inquire more about the details of what caused Hannah's death, but she didn't ask. She covered her astonishment by immediately searching through the cassette tapes.

"We'd like something that is not familiar to most people. Do you know of any songs that were written specifically with a child's death in mind?" I asked.

"No, I don't know of anything like that, but I'm willing to help you look if you want me to."

"Yes, that would be helpful. We've been out taking care of the arrangements all day and would like to get home soon. It's been a long two days and we're tired."

The clerk pulled out several selections and passed them to me. I looked over the lyrics first and then listened to the music in order to test it for the suitability of our situation. I listened to four or five songs and rejected them all; the words were appropriate, but the music was not delicate and pleasing to the ear. Nothing I heard reminded me of Hannah at all.

Phil came over to check on my progress. He was successful at finding a small white Bible for Hannah to hold in the casket. It was just what I had pictured.

"Do you want to help us look for music?" I asked Phil. "We're having a hard time finding anything."

"Sure. What exactly are you looking for?" he asked.

I explained my expectations for both the lyrics and the music. "I know that I'm asking a lot, but this part of the funeral is very important to me. I want the song we choose to express our love for Hannah and heartache in missing her, yet also the joy we have in knowing that we will see her again someday."

I was so thankful that Phil didn't show any impatience with my request. He sensed how passionate I was about finding the perfect song. Despite his fatigue, Phil began to look through the CD section without complaint.

After several more rejections and growing disappointment that such a song did not exist, the clerk passed me the tape of a song by Kathy Troccoli entitled "Good-Bye For Now." Later I learned that she wrote it for a friend whose young child had passed away.

"I think this is exactly what you are looking for," the clerk smiled.

After reading the lyrics I was convinced. Tears rolled down my face as I listened to the melody. "It's perfect," I said quietly.

The Lord, knowing my heart's desire, granted my request and led us to this song. I've included the words below because they summarize the feelings I had about Hannah's death so simply and poetically.

> I can't believe that you're really gone now.
> Seems like it's all just a dream.
> How can it be that the world will go on
> when something has died within me?

> Leaves will turn, and my heart will burn with colors of you.
> Snow will fall but I'll recall your warmth.
> Summer wind, breathing in your memory;
> I'll miss you.

Chorus:
But there will be time when I'll see your face
and I'll hear your voice
and there we will laugh again.
And there will come a day when I'll hold you close;
no more tears to cry, 'cause we'll have forever.
But I'll say good-bye for now.

I can't imagine my life without you.
You held a place all your own.
Just knowing you were beneath the same sky.
Oh, what a joy I have known.

On rainy days, in many ways you'll water my heart.
On starry nights, I'll glimpse the light of your smile.
Never far from my heart, you'll stay with me.
So I'll wait.

I asked Carmen to be the soloist at Hannah's funeral, and she graciously obliged. I apologized many times for giving her such a tough assignment—who could possibly sing that song and maintain their composure? I knew Carmen was the ideal person to handle the pressure. She would pray for the Lord's strength to help her sing it without crying. Her beautiful voice would sweetly convey my grieving but hopeful heart that we would see Hannah again.

Long after the funeral, the Lord continued using this song to minister to me. Phil and I hummed the tune endlessly as we went about our day. The song track became a permanent fixture in the cassette player for weeks. Every so often Phil would say to me, "Go play Hannah's song," and we stopped our activity long enough to listen and remember her. Throughout this ordeal, God provided comfort to our hurting souls in unique ways. The song "Good-Bye For Now" was a means of grace that He used to help us to cope with Hannah's death.

After a quick stop at Wal-Mart to pick up three rolls of developed film, we finally headed for home. The pictures of Hannah were the most recent of her, and we needed them to assemble photo boards for the visitation and funeral. While driving home, we glanced through the pictures as "Good-Bye For Now" played on the car stereo. Every photo of Hannah showed her smiling. She was so happy to be part of our family, and she loved her sisters and brothers wholeheartedly. God had provided Hannah with such a wonderful life while here on earth.

We came home after 5 p.m. to a full house. Phil's parents had arrived from Florida, along with Aunt Linda. (Uncle Jim, Linda's husband, had decided to stay behind, a decision he later regretted but accepted as God's providence.) Norm, Janine, and their three children had also come to visit with the family. Patti had everything under control and wasn't the least bit overwhelmed by having to care for the ten children who played wildly under our roof. It seemed like Moriah, Nathan, and Abigail were enjoying the company of their cousins, which I was glad about. Everything that was normal for them had suddenly been turned upside down.

That evening, Patti, Phil's mom, and Aunt Linda prepared dinner and cared for the children. Aunt Loretta (Mom Dufrin's sister), and her husband, Uncle George, came to visit with us all the way from Windsor, Canada. They spent several hours with our family and left in the late evening. Phil's parents departed for home shortly thereafter and promised to come back with Aunt Linda at 7:30 the next morning to get breakfast underway and greet the children when they awoke. By 9:00 that night the house was empty of guests, and we were alone as a family.

The following day was Tuesday, and we had no funeral plans to make or anywhere to go. Mom and Aunt Linda arrived right on time, and Phil arose to welcome them.

I was awake but had no motivation to get out of bed. Nathan peeked through the open doorway, and I beckoned him to come join me in bed. We snuggled together without saying a word. Was he thinking about Hannah much like I was? Neither Moriah nor Nathan had shown a great deal emotion since the day we told them. Perhaps there was just enough distraction around our house to keep them from dwelling on the loss of their sister. For the time it was what they needed.

With no set plans for the day, Phil and I did whatever felt best to comfort our weary souls. Patti, Norm, Janine and the kids all returned and were there to fill in for us whenever we needed to talk on the phone, read e-mail messages, or just be alone.

139

That afternoon Phil escaped for several hours into our bedroom. When I finally realized he had not been around for quite some time, I went upstairs and found him making the finishing touches on a poem he had written to Hannah.

"What have you been doing up here?" I quietly asked upon entering our bedroom.

"I wrote a poem—for Hannah. Can I read it to you?"

In the past year Phil had developed a real love for the written word in poetic form, so this was not the first poem that he had written. I enjoyed all his other works and usually broke into tears when reading them.

"Are you trying to make me cry?" I joked warmly. "Your poems always make me cry."

"No, I was just trying to get some of these mixed-up thoughts out of my head and make sense of them on paper."

The words of Phil's "Letter to Hannah" were so plainly written, yet eloquently exposed the pain of a father who, too soon in life, had to trust his precious daughter into the hands of God.

My Dearest Hannah,

Never in my wildest dreams
Did I imagine this day might be.
When I would see you to your grave
And suffer such pain and grief.

Yet on this earth no resting place
Is found for your sweet soul.
For heaven bound you go today
To Him who makes you whole.

Remember Him, the Lord our God,
Sweet Jesus is His name.
The One we sang and spoke about
And prayed for us to change.

Now changed you are no more to cry
Or suffer from sin's pain.
Complete in Him who died for us,
Christ has become your gain.

Oh, how I ache for one more day,
One more hug and kiss.
Or one more game of Scoops to play,
Your laugh, your voice, I miss.

But God has chosen otherwise
And in His will I rest.
That I should know you four short years
And count it for my best.

Never to walk you down the aisle
For marriage with a man.
Instead to join you as a bride,
Our wedding with the Lamb.

I miss you, Hannah, more each day
Mere words cannot express.
But I will see you very soon
Before His throne of righteousness.

Love,
Daddy

In the silence of our bedroom, Phil rolled up a copy of his poem and used the pink ribbon last worn in Hannah's hair to tie it closed. Originally meant for only Hannah to "read," he planned to place the scroll next to her body in the casket to be buried with her forever. But after listening to Phil read the poem, I encouraged him to also place a framed copy on display at Hannah's visitation. Phil was reluctant to do so, but I insisted, knowing that it would minister the love and grace of God to those who read the words.

Giving Hannah the gift of a beautiful dress to wear and flowers to cover the casket helped me to find closure in my role as a mother. Writing that poem was Phil's gift to his daughter. It was his way of relinquishing the role of provider and protector over to our Lord, whom he trusted would do this in his place. Phil always knew who Hannah's real Father was and didn't question His ability to oversee the heart and soul of our little girl. This act of love through the written word helped Phil to "give Hannah away," joining her to Christ as a bride.

Throughout the day and night we received an abundance of phone calls, and a multitude of people stopped by to visit with us. Phil and I welcomed their company, not wanting to be alone just yet. Personally, I was scared to face an empty house. The distraction of family and friends was helpful in easing my pain a little. When left alone I would have to confront the full weight of my grief. Would I be able to bear it? How would I possibly take care of the other children? I had little energy to be concerned with them, and I greatly depended on the help of our family. Even nursing little eight-month-old Samuel was too much. I made the decision to stop nursing him, knowing that this would make him less dependent on me in the next days and weeks to come.

Several of my girlfriends had stopped by on Tuesday evening to talk with me. We sat on my bedroom floor and listened to "Good-Bye For Now," pouring over Hannah's scrapbooks and drowning our sorrows in a bag of M&M's! Their presence ministered to my heart. Throughout the day I wanted to talk about Hannah but kept myself from bringing her up in order to keep the mood light. However, these friends listened intently and encouraged me to talk openly about Hannah's life and death. When the last friend departed, I felt a little less burdened.

Going to bed that night was difficult as thoughts of the upcoming visitation kept my mind active. In a strange way I looked forward to seeing Hannah again, even if I could not hold her as before. There was something comforting about just being near her body. Drifting off to sleep, I silently prayed that God would give me the strength to glorify Him as I spoke with the hundreds of people who would be coming to Hannah's visitation. *May our faith in Christ be that which draws people near to You. Please give us the strength to be bold witnesses of Your grace and mercy.*

Phil and I wanted people to notice something different about the way we responded to Hannah's death. God calls us to be strangers and aliens in this world. Would our testimony be an example of this truth? Because of our daughter's death, would those who didn't know Christ begin to question their own assurance of salvation? For those who did know Christ, would our God-glorifying response to suffering cause them to value the things of this earth a little bit less and think about eternity a little bit more?

Tomorrow's visitation would give us an opportunity to share the goodness and mercy of Christ with those who would not ordinarily listen. We expected it to be an exhausting task but were certain that the Lord would give us the physical and emotional strength to endure it.

∿

"There is a slight delay in our preparations for the visitation," Mike told us once we arrived at the funeral home. "We had a funeral this morning and have been working ever since then to be ready by one o'clock."

"We're in no hurry," assured Phil. "Please take all the time you need."

"Well, there is one other thing. I'm not satisfied with the way Hannah looks. Her makeup isn't quite right. I've called in our best artist from Lansing to come and fix it, but he won't be here for another twenty minutes."

"Again, don't worry about it. We'd rather she look good, even if it shortens our time. Is there a private place separate from the lobby where we can wait?" asked Phil.

"Thank you for understanding," Mike sighed with relief. "Yes, you and your wife can wait in this room and close the door behind you."

Phil and I wanted to be alone and not stressed by the burden of having to make small talk. We asked our family to take care of the children for us while we waited in the other room. Sitting on the stairs just inside the lobby door, we watched the funeral home staff work frantically to carry in load after load of flowers, all for our Hannah Marie.

The makeup artist arrived after fifteen minutes and walked quickly in front of us without looking our way. Five minutes later he exited from the room and passed by briskly, this time glancing in our direction. *How many children has this man attended to throughout his lifetime?* I wondered to myself. *Does the death of a child affect him, or is this just a matter of business?*

Mike went into Hannah's viewing room one last time to make sure the preparations were set. He opened the partition which separated the waiting room and said, "Everything is ready. You can go see her now."

Phil carried the scroll of his poem in one hand and the Bible in the other. I held a plastic bag of bright pink rose petals that would be placed around Hannah's body. I instantly noticed how small the casket was.

We approached Hannah's body, put our arms around one another and stared at our lifeless daughter.

Through quiet tears I daintily lay the rose petals around Hannah's upper body, and Phil slipped the Bible under her hands. "Look at the bracelet around her wrist," I said. "It's perfect."

Phil tucked the poem next to Hannah's body in an inconspicuous place. I continued to stare at her dress, sweater, and hair. Everything looked just the way I wanted it to, except for her hair. The ribbon that we provided was not what they used but was from the hospital instead. For an instant I thought about asking Mike if I could change the ribbon but decided that Hannah's hair wasn't important right now—spending time with her alone, was.

Hannah's makeup did not look natural at all, especially her lips. I didn't know if this was normal—perhaps all deceased people looked that way. Overall, Hannah looked good to me, the only difference being that she didn't have her usual smile. Maybe this is why she didn't appear more natural.

After a few minutes passed, we were ready to let our children come see Hannah. Mike helped escort them in while I stood near the casket to greet them. Phil picked up Abigail, and I drew Moriah and Nathan close to me, one on each side. Together the five us approached Hannah's casket.

"This is just Hannah's body. Her spirit is now living with Jesus in heaven," I told them. "Doesn't she look beautiful?"

Moriah and Nathan nodded their heads in agreement. They were speechless. What could I say that would help them through this?

We stood together for several minutes, each of us trying to grapple with the reality of Hannah's death. The Hannah we knew was not in that body. Yes, she was in heaven, but where exactly is that? Could she see down to earth and know we were viewing her body? With so many thoughts running through my mind, I was too confused to even cry.

The time was nearing 2 p.m., so we called for our relatives to come in next. Each person who came forward remarked on how beautiful Hannah looked, and I soaked it all in. Pride for my daughter began to well up in me instead of tears. I smiled and hugged each one with an amazing strength. God was answering my prayers, giving me what was needed to provide comfort to our family members, both the saved and unsaved.

With just five minutes to spare, Phil and I had a chance to walk around the room to see from whom all the flowers came. I was pleased with how the flowers we had chosen for Hannah were arranged. Bouquets and baskets of flowers continued to stream in all throughout the evening. We counted thirty-six different arrangements, most of which were cheery and bright and not the usual funeral-type flower. The sunflowers, daises, tulips, and small rose buds were among our favorites. It may seem petty, but I was secretly glad that Hannah had been given so many flowers.

Looking over the room I noticed everything we asked to be displayed was perfectly arranged: a picture of Hannah on a pedestal near the casket, a large black and white photograph of our family (taken only the week before), and two large felt boards mounted with numerous photos of Hannah at all stages of life. On small end tables throughout the parlor sat Hannah's scrapbooks, the framed copy of Phil's poem, and a copy of Hannah's ultrasound picture, taken at eight months gestational age, with a portion of Psalm 139 printed at the bottom: *"For you created my inmost being; you knit me together in my mother's womb. I praise you because I am fearfully and wonderfully made . . . All the days ordained for me we were written in your book before one of them came to be"* (Psalm 139:13-14, 16).

Just the day before, I came across this ultrasound picture while looking through Hannah's box of memorabilia. I decided to display a framed copy of it at the visitation as a proclamation of our faith in a sovereign God who had planned all of Hannah's days from birth to death. In spite of her many challenges and physical limitations, God was the One who put Hannah together that way for a purpose. We hoped that these truths might minister to people who harbored resentment towards God for not answering their prayers of healing for Hannah.

At exactly 2 p.m. the people slowly started to arrive, and soon a long line formed down the center aisle of the room. We hadn't planned to greet each person individually while standing near Hannah's casket, but it just turned out that way. Although tiring at times (especially while wearing two-inch heels), we appreciated the opportunity to individually minister to each person and display the glory of God through our words. This was a direct answer to the prayer I had spoken the night before.

The line of people waiting to see us didn't let up until almost five o'clock. As the last person left, Phil and I dropped our weary bodies in two chairs and sat quietly, gazing from a distance at Hannah's body.

"That went well, don't you think?" asked Phil.

"I am overwhelmed by the number of people who came. There were so many people that I did not expect."

"Yeah, I had a hard time remembering some of their names!" (This has always been a struggle for Phil anyway, regardless of the circumstances.)

Becky encouraged us to walk down the street to Norm and Janine's house in order to eat dinner. A large gathering of people had congregated at their home, and everyone enjoyed the wonderful food provided by the people in our church. I plopped down into the sofa and did not move again until an hour later when we went back to the funeral home for the next visitation starting at 6 p.m.

The second visitation was much the same as the first— people lined up and were willing to wait an hour to see us. The assistant from the funeral home gently kept telling us, "Hurry along. There are many people waiting. Tell them, 'Thank you for coming,' and then move on to the next person."

Impossible! Many of the guests were people we had not seen or spoken to in years. There wouldn't be time to catch up on everything we had missed, but we didn't want to be rude and rush them through either!

Phil and I saw this as an opportunity to proclaim Christ. We weren't shy about professing from Whom our strength came. I said things to people about their relationship with God that I've never possessed the boldness to share. I didn't care about offending anyone. When one man came forward to talk with us he commented, "Your faith has kept you so strong."

My reply took both of us by surprise: "You can have the same faith if you would follow Christ instead of the things of this world. You might have a lot of money, but none of that will buy your way into heaven. You can't take any of this stuff with you."

Now that's bold!

Perhaps some thought Phil and I were crazy because, after all, we had just lost our daughter—it was to be expected. But I heard numerous comments from both Christians and non-Christians who said that our faith was amazing. "How are they doing that?" they asked. "They are comforting other people instead of us comforting them!"

We were only doing what God had given us the grace and strength to do. I felt so much genuine joy—how was that possible? My daughter's body laid in a casket just six feet away, and I was smiling and laughing instead of crying. Such an amazing response like that can only come from the grace of an amazing God.

When the last person left, the time was 9 p.m. Our children had been kindly tended to for seven straight hours by both relatives and friends. Now it was time to gather them up and say good-bye to Hannah for the last time.

The rest of our family waited outside the room behind the partition. They knew this would be a difficult time and encouraged us to take as long as we needed.

Moriah let some of her emotion show as she sobbed close to the casket. She appeared to understand more than the others what this final good-bye meant. Moriah's tears prompted me to cry, and Phil was doing his best to be a strong comfort to the women in his life. He gently spoke reassuring words into Moriah's ear, and she nodded her head in agreement with his utterances. Nathan appeared undisturbed but quiet, and Abigail was frantically trying to get down out of my arms.

When the children finished saying good-bye to their sister, we escorted them to the waiting area and then were left alone with Hannah. I was so exhausted after a long day of visiting that the full weight of the moment didn't hit me. Neither of us needed much time; by the grace of God we were ready to let her go. I enjoyed being near Hannah throughout the day. The next time I would see her again would be in heaven. Such a long time to wait . . . .

Just before we were ready to leave, Abigail tugged at my hand and began to pull away from me. "I want to see Hannah again!" she whined.

Having no strength left to argue, I consented. "OK, Abigail. You can see Hannah one more time, but that is all. It's late, and we have to go home now."

Abigail pulled free of my hand and ran down the aisle toward Hannah's casket as I trailed behind her. When Abigail reached the casket, I immediately became alarmed that she might grab on to the side in order to see Hannah better. I envisioned the entire casket flipping over onto the floor . . . .

"Abigail, don't touch!" I hollered, hurrying to prevent a disaster. By now I was within several feet and could hear these precious, final words spoken to her sister and best friend:

"See you in heaven, OK?"

I heaved a sigh of relief, and my face broke into a smile. Perhaps she did understand more than we gave her credit for. Without another word, Abigail turned and sprinted back to the lobby.

Although it was just like Abigail to cause a scene, I hadn't expected her to put the "icing" on such a joyous day!

7
A Time to Mourn

Blessed are those who mourn,
for they will be comforted.

Matthew 5:3

"SANDY, ARE YOU ALMOST READY TO GO?" PHIL CALLED TO me from the bottom of the stairs. "We have to leave in five minutes if we are going to make it to the church by noon."

"I'll be down in just a minute. We're almost done up here."

Alyssa, a friend from church who works as a hair stylist, offered to come over and fix Moriah and Abigail's hair for the funeral. At the last minute we decided to curl my hair also. I was grateful that this was one aspect of getting ready I didn't have to worry about.

Patti and her family also arrived early to help take care of children and pack a bag for Samuel. Without her help I could not have put everyone together on time. Emotional stress puts a strain on the ability to organize and think clearly, two things that are crucial for getting a family of six people out the door.

We arrived at a church a little after 12 p.m. There were already several cars in the parking lot, mostly belonging to the people of Covenant Life. We had told them to come early if they wanted to sit near the front during the memorial service.

Once inside the building, a staff member from the funeral home directed us to the sanctuary. Hannah's closed casket was positioned near the front with several flower arrangements surrounding it. Mike had saved some of the rose petals and encouraged me to place them on the top. No one was present in the sanctuary at the time, so I walked to the front and strategically placed the petals one by one. Since we had already said good-bye to Hannah the night before, we didn't feel the need to stay near her casket until the funeral began. Besides this, people were beginning to arrive, and we wanted to be out of sight until one o'clock. We exited through a door at the front of the church which led us down a stairway and into the basement where preparations for the funeral dinner were underway.

Every woman from our congregation was working in the kitchen. Carmen met us at the basement door and showed us all that they had done to prepare for the meal. The large, open room was set up with long tables that were covered in white tablecloths. Each table adorned two centerpieces of yellow daffodils planted in white clay pots. Thick purple and yellow strips of ribbon sat underneath each pot and streamed down the tables. Laying at each place setting was a set of utensils and a bookmark with a message written by Carmen's husband, Ben. It read:

Jesus said, *"Let the little children come to me, and do not hinder them, for the kingdom of heaven belongs to such as these."* Hannah Marie Dufrin belongs, having never been hindered from seeing the exaltation of Christ. The truth of Titus 3:4-6 has been portrayed most precious: *"But when the kindness and love of God our Savior appeared, he saved us, not because of the righteous things we had done, but because of his mercy. He saved us through the washing of rebirth and renewal by the Holy Spirit, whom he poured out on us generously through Jesus Christ our Savior. . . ."* If the portals of heaven could be rolled back and we could see the all encompassing glory of Jesus that Hannah now revels in, we believe she would cry out with wholehearted voice, "It is not about my death, but His. It is not about my life but about His life that was given in my place! For Christ has made a way!" *"For it is by grace you have been saved, through faith—and this not from yourselves, it is the gift of God . . ."* (Ephesians 2:8). *"For God so loved the world that he* gave *his one and only Son, that whoever believes in him shall not perish but have eternal life"* (John 3:16). So may God bless you dear, sweet Hannah as you are safe within His arms. Amen.

"Everything we planned for today was with you in mind, Sandy," said Carmen. "We know how much you pay attention to detail, and so we have done the same in honor of you."

I was truly astounded by the amount of work that went into planning an event of this size on such short notice. No one would have believed that our small church was capable of organizing it in just three days time.

"This is more than I ever could have asked for. Thank you." I said.

"Oh, I almost forgot. Here is one more detail that we added in honor of Hannah." Carmen reached into a flower pot and pulled out a two-inch cardboard Strawberry Shortcake figurine. "There is one hiding in every pot!"

"You guys are too much!" I exclaimed. The decorations reminded me so much of Hannah; it seemed as though they were meant for her wedding rather than her funeral. It blessed me to see their excitement in making these preparations, all out of love for our family. How would I ever repay their thoughtfulness?

While waiting for the service to begin, Phil and I stayed in the basement, keeping ourselves hidden. A few people happened to stumble upon us and asked how we were doing.

"We're doing well," I replied. "I'm actually looking forward to the service with eagerness and excitement."

I'm certain this is not the answer anyone expected. There was nothing phony about my response; I meant it most sincerely. We had predicted that over 300 people would come to Hannah's funeral. Of these 300, in our estimation close to half of them did not know Christ as their Lord and Savior. It was our responsibility to be messengers of the good news, and that is what we intended to do. Phil and I both wanted the gospel to be preached strongly during the service, and we trusted that the Spirit would move in the hearts of those whom He would save.

At a funeral most people begin to think a lot more about their own mortality. If they don't have the assurance of knowing where they will spend eternity, they will start asking questions as a result. We saw Hannah's funeral as an opportunity to share the reason for our hope and to provide answers to the questions that God was stirring up in people's hearts.

We had asked Ben Harmon's father, Tom, to officiate the memorial service. Tom is an itinerant preacher who travels from church to church all across the United States, sharing the gospel in a dynamic way. We first heard Tom preach about eight years before while attending a family camp in northern Michigan. His love for God, the Word, and passion for the gospel had been evident upon hearing the first words uttered from his mouth.

Tom sat down with us to go over the order for the service, making sure he remembered exactly what we had planned. First, Phil and I would speak to the people ourselves. It had been Tom's idea for us to give our testimony, and we agreed to it almost immediately. This was another occasion to bring glory to Christ's name through our affliction. We wanted people to hear from us personally how God's grace had helped us through the last four days. It would be more convincing coming from the parents of the child who had died rather than from the preacher who was expected to says things like that.

Norm and Ron came down to the basement to inform us that the service would start in five minutes. Tom led the five of us in prayer, and then Phil and I walked together with Moriah and Nathan up the stairs. Abigail and Samuel were being cared for by others which I was so appreciative of. Both of them had woken up with colds that morning and were more irritable and tired than usual.

When we walked through the door and into the sanctuary, I glanced up and noticed that the church was almost full. The four of us took a seat in the front row, and our families sat in the rows behind us. Across the aisle were the people from our church whom I consider to be family as well. I was pleased they had secured a place near the front and were all sitting together. Beyond this I'm not sure where any one person was seated in particular. All eyes were fixed upon our family, and if I had looked up to survey the room, I probably would have smiled. Most people cry at funerals, and those who don't are thought to be in denial. I continued looking forward or stared down at the floor.

The service began shortly after 1 p.m. with a greeting by Tom and the singing of two hymns: "How Great Thou Art" and "Come Thou Fount." Singing those songs brought me the closest to heaven that I will ever experience while here on earth! The Spirit's presence was so real to me that I cried for joy while reflecting on the peace Hannah now had with Christ. I couldn't help but lift my hands in praise to my Lord and King who had mercy on me, a sinner. If the feelings I had were just a taste of what we will experience in heaven, what a glorious place it will be!

Following the hymns, Tom introduced Kristi who had been asked to give Hannah's eulogy. Having been labeled "Hannah's Second Mother," we knew she was the right person to share how God used Hannah's life to glorify Him.

She began the speech by saying, "We have told Phil and Sandy many times that we would do anything for them, so when they asked me if I would come before you and share about Hannah and who she was, I felt honored and privileged."

Kristi spoke about Hannah's life from before birth, through all of her medical challenges, and about the love she had for her siblings. She told us how much Hannah had touched the lives of everyone who met her and how the fruits of the Spirit were evident in her life, even at the young age of four.

Hannah was pure joy. She smiled at you with her whole body. Her big brown eyes were filled with delight when she looked at you. It made you feel good all over. Her dimples were charming, and when she laughed you couldn't help but laugh with her. And that hair—that luscious hair. Hannah loved her hair, and so did we. It was impossible not to.

Hannah had peace. She never questioned her physical problems and rarely complained about what things she had to endure for the sake of her health care. She was a tough little girl. She would fall down and more often than not, would get up without any tears or recognition from anyone.

She had patience, kindness, goodness, faithfulness, gentleness and self-control, all wrapped up in a package. She was the first one to give up her way if we needed to choose someone to go first in a game or with a toy. And she was the first one to apologize and give hugs if involved in a squabble. She forgave so quickly and so willingly. If only we could all have that said about us.

Hannah was easy to love, and people were drawn to her. This makes it all the more difficult to lose her and to understand why now, when she was doing so well. But the pain is beginning to soften, and the understanding is beginning to come. Jesus said in John 12:24, *"I tell you the truth, unless a kernel of wheat falls to the ground and dies, it remains only a single seed. But if it dies, it produces many seeds."*

Hannah's life has continually drawn people together in amazing ways and has bridged gaps that seemed impossible to bridge. Her life facilitated growth among believers, and because of this, people without faith in Jesus have been drawn to hear more about Him. Without ever knowing it, she has had an incredible impact on my life.

I miss you so much, Hannah, and I am so glad that I got to love you so much!

Kristi's eloquent words accurately portrayed who Hannah was and how God used her life to impact others. I could not have written a better tribute to Hannah myself.

Following the eulogy, Carmen stepped forward to sing "Good-Bye For Now." While listening to Kristi speak I had held myself together quite well. But upon hearing this song, I struggled to contain my emotions. To keep myself from breaking down, I quietly sang along with Carmen as if I were singing to Hannah in heaven.

When Carmen finished, Phil's father read two Scripture passages. Since Phil and I were scheduled to speak next, I'm glad we had a few minutes to collect ourselves before facing the people.

Tom introduced us by explaining how it was arranged for Phil and I to speak:

In talking with Phil on the phone about the order of today's service, he began to share with me some things that God was doing in their lives as a result of Hannah's death. I asked him if he would be willing to share these revelations with all of you. How many of you know that this is a hard thing to ask a parent to do at their daughter's funeral? Phil told me that he would talk to Sandy and then pray about it.

When Phil had approached me with the possibility of giving our testimonies during the funeral, I said yes without hesitation. Hard as it might be to speak about, our words would be a powerful witness of God's sovereignty, helping others to view Hannah's death from an eternal perspective rather than as a "tragedy."

Phil spoke first and shared what the Lord had revealed to him through Isaiah 46.

The day following Hannah's death, thoughts started to enter my mind—thoughts that were accusing and thoughts that asked, "What if the surgeons hadn't met with us in December to discuss her case? What if there hadn't been an emergency that caused February 6 to open up for the surgeon? What if you hadn't pushed for that earlier date? What if Hannah's surgery hadn't been bumped to later in the day? What if you had just walked out of the hospital and said, 'Not yet'?"

I prayed for God to forgive me for such thoughts but also to give me something to hold on to for strength. This is the text that I was given early Monday morning:

> *Listen to me, O house of Jacob,*
> *all you who remain of the house of Israel,*
> *you whom I have upheld since you*
> *were conceived,*
> *and have carried since your birth.*
> *Even to your old age and gray hairs*
> *I am he, I am he who will sustain you.*
> *I have made you and I will carry you;*
> *I will sustain you and I will rescue you.*

Isaiah 46:3-4

> *Remember this, fix it in your mind,*
> *take it to heart, you rebels.*
> *Remember the former things, those of long ago;*
> *I am God, and there is no other;*
> *I am God, and there is none like me.*
> *I make known the end from the beginning,*
> *from ancient times, what is still to come.*
> *I say: My purpose will stand,*
> *and I will do all that I please.*

From the east I summon a bird of prey;
from a far-off land, a man to fulfill my purpose.
What I have said, that I will bring about;
what I have planned, that will I do.

Isaiah 46:8-11

Some may ask, "Where is the comfort in these words?" Let me tell you about my God.

He is sovereign over all His creation, and His will is not only perfect but it is sure. Many rely on chance or fear its consequences. Will I get cancer? What are my chances of getting in a car accident? What is the probability that the surgery will be a success?

I have no such fears nor is my confidence in things such as statistics. Know today that Hannah's conception, birth, life, and death were not just known by God, but purposed by Him. The words "tragedy," "misfortune," or "bad luck" are not in my vocabulary.

Hannah is where I want to be and will be by the grace of God. I have no fear for the future because indeed He has spoken it; He will also bring it to pass. He has purposed it; He will also do it.

Now it was my turn to testify how God was sustaining us through this trial and to encourage those who didn't know Christ to trust Him with their lives. I began by sharing about how God changed my heart at the age of 18.

Many of you are just like I was—you know who God is, you go to church, and you are even able to quote some Scriptures. Yet you haven't fully surrendered your life to Christ, living for Him instead of for yourself. After I speak, Mr. Harmon is going to come forward and share with you the good news of Jesus Christ and how you can truly attain eternal life. Please listen with your whole heart, and if God impresses upon you to make a change in your life, do it and don't be afraid of what could happen. He will sustain you through whatever trial comes your way. You will have a joy inexpressible as you walk on this earth, and it will carry you through anything, just as it has for us during this time.

We don't want people to walk away from this funeral being just better people, desiring to do good. No, we are praying that your hearts will be changed for eternity, and that your faith in Jesus Christ will be stronger.

From the time Hannah was a baby, we knew she had been born for a purpose. We gave her to God and trusted His plan. We still do, even in her death. God had planned that He would be most glorified in her death than in her life. We can honestly say that her death is worth one life saved for eternity. Will it be your life? Will you trust His plan?

Many people have marveled at our strength through this ordeal. In the Scriptures it talks about Jesus' disciples counting it all joy to suffer for the sake of Christ. I never quite understood what that meant or how they could have such faith in the face of persecution and death. Well, in the face of our daughter's death, I can understand the joy they felt a little bit better. It has been a privilege to suffer in this way for the sake of my Lord. He has given us what we need to bear this burden. We know without a doubt that someday we will be with Hannah again. Yes, she is in a better place, not because she doesn't have pain or sorrow, but because she is in the presence of Christ for eternity!

We are honored to have been chosen by God to bear this burden, and we feel so undeserving to have been given Hannah for four years. Thank you for all of your prayers and words of encouragement. We are praying for you all, too. We encourage you to look to Christ as your all in all. May Hannah's death not be in vain.

Were the words Phil and I spoke truly heartfelt, or were we pretending to be strong because it was the "right" response that a Christian should have? Without qualification, we genuinely meant every word and didn't have to fake our strength, realizing that *it was the work of God's grace in our hearts that allowed us to think and feel in this way.* There was no "secret inner strength" that freed us from the "normal" reaction of someone whose daughter had died.

Does this mean that we never were sad or didn't struggle to make sense out of God's plan? Certainly not! For weeks and months following Hannah's death, I cried several times a day because I missed her so much. There were moments when thoughts of *Why Hannah?* or *This isn't fair!* entered my mind. Those were Satan's attempts to pull us away from God, and we recognized his schemes. The temptation to dive into self-pity and depression was great at times, but we made the choice to say no to the lure of Satan and yes to following God, even if it seemed like more than we could handle.

The funeral service commenced with the presentation of the gospel as given by Tom. His usual energetic style did not suit the somber mood of a funeral, and we were glad it didn't. Hannah was in heaven because of Christ's work on the cross, and that was something to rejoice about!

At the end of the sermon Tom asked the congregation to pray with him and respond to the gospel if God was leading them. He didn't expect anyone to raise their hand or come forward; this was a private matter between God and the heart of a man.

We will never know the full impact of Hannah's funeral on the people who attended. Was anyone saved? What seeds were planted? Phil and I had the privilege to hear several testimonies of how God had worked in people's hearts, but the final conclusions will have to wait until we reach heaven ourselves.

To close the service we chose the well-known hymn "It is Well With My Soul." Originally this was not the first song we had selected. Two days before the funeral I had sat down at the piano to play a few arrangements. Patti was standing nearby, singing along with me. She asked, "Do you know how to play 'It is Well With My Soul'?" While singing the words I realized what a declaration this was of our faith in Christ. The second and fourth verses were especially meaningful:

> Though Satan should buffet, though trials should come,
> Let this blest assurance control,
> That Christ has regarded my helpless estate,
> And hath shed His own blood for my soul.

> And, Lord, haste the day when the faith shall be sight,
> The clouds be rolled back as a scroll,
> The trump shall resound and the Lord shall descend,
> "Even so" it is well with my soul.

I played the last note and looked over at Phil who was listening from the couch. "What do you think about using this hymn for the last song in the service?"

He agreed without hesitation. "I'll call Ron and ask him to make the change."

Following the hymn, two members of the funeral staff walked to the front and began wheeling Hannah's casket back down the aisle. Walking behind Hannah's casket, Phil and I held hands and looked at each other with huge smiles. The memorial service turned out exactly as we had planned—Hannah was sweetly remembered, God's faithfulness was proclaimed, and best of all the gospel was preached! There was no containing our joy!

Several people commented that it looked as though we had floated out of the sanctuary. One young woman, who had never attended a funeral before, asked her mother, "Am I supposed to feel this good after a funeral? Are all funerals this way?"

There is no other explanation for our joy other than the Spirit's presence and God's grace upon us.

Once Hannah's casket was taken out of the sanctuary, the casket bearers picked it up and began carrying it outside. We thought it would be appropriate if Nathan, along with Hannah's cousins—Ian, Doug, and C.J—were given this job. Hannah's uncles, Norm and Doug, helped the young boys by holding the front and back for added support. The rose petals I had placed on top of the casket fell along the sidewalk, marking the way to the hearse. Watching from the door of the church, Phil began to weep. It was difficult for him to see his little girl being carried away to her final resting place.

Given the number of people who attended Hannah's funeral, the director escorted our family to the limousine to wait until the church cleared out. If we had taken the time to thank everyone for coming, we would have been delayed at least another hour.

Abigail and Samuel were brought to the limousine and strapped into their car seats behind us. Phil and I watched through the tinted glass windows as people exited the building. We were blessed by the various individuals who gave up their afternoon to come to our daughter's funeral. Other than our immediate families, those who came included: people from Phil's work (who drew straws to see who would have to stay behind), people from the church we attended as college students, pastors of various churches in the area, members of the board of directors at the crisis pregnancy center where I served, hospital staff, therapists, neighbors, friends from high school, and people from far-away places such as Ohio, Illinois, Wisconsin, Louisiana, Georgia, and Canada. Regrettably, we were not able to speak with many of those people, personally thanking them for their love and support.

When I asked one of the staff how long he expected the funeral procession to be, he replied, "We stopped counting cars at seventy." While driving to the cemetery ten miles away, I tried looking out the window to see where the procession ended but could not see that far back.

The "Parade for Princess Hannah" (as the Calhoun family named it) was a long and slow drive. Our mood was light and merry as we marveled at the number of people who followed us. The kids were content and quiet while munching on the peanuts and cheese that Patti had thought to pack for us. Phil and I were still fired up about the funeral and couldn't restrain our joy. We even tried witnessing to the limo driver on the way to the cemetery!

Driving into Williamston we noticed an elderly gentleman standing on the sidewalk, holding his hat to his chest out of respect for the passing procession. Although he didn't know our family, his gesture displayed heartfelt sympathy and compassion. Tears came to my eyes when I observed this act of honor towards my daughter.

It took some time for everyone to park and walk to Hannah's grave site. Our family stayed in the limo until the majority of the people had caught up to us. Abigail was growing impatient and asked if we could go to Caesarland after the cemetery. Even after I said no and explained the reason why several times, she wouldn't let up. I was thankful when Mike motioned for us to get out of the car and walk over to the grave site.

The snow had been cleared away, and the tent was set up around Hannah's grave with five chairs lined up in a row underneath it. The casket bearers carried her casket over to the tent and placed it on the metal support above the grave. We sat down and waited for the remaining people to file in around us.

When the graveside service began, Samuel started to get fussy, and it was hard for me to hear much of the Scripture that Tom was reading. After a while I became annoyed with Samuel's crying and turned to pass him off to Patti who was standing behind me. Not long after that, Tom concluded his thoughts and invited the people to come back to the church to join us for the meal. He also asked them to be patient in waiting for us to return to the church so that we could spend time alone with Hannah at the cemetery.

We waited about five minutes for the crowd to return to their cars. Phil and I stood up with the children and approached Hannah's casket. Although we had already said good-bye after the visitation, we were permitted one last chance to make it final.

I had no more words to express to my departed daughter. It seemed more fitting to sing our farewell instead. "Let's sing 'Hannah's Song' to her one more time," I suggested.

Through a wellspring of tears, we sang softly while caressing the casket. "Hannah Marie-a, sweet Hannah Marie-a, how I love you. Hannah Marie-a, my Hannah Marie-a, how I love you."

I plucked the remaining flowers from the top of the casket and let them fall one by one into the hole where Hannah would be laid to rest. "Your final resting place has been christened with flowers," I told her. Leaning over and gently kissing the casket, I said, "Good-bye, my love. See you soon."

Walking away from the grave site was more difficult than I had anticipated. I was torn inside. It didn't seem right to leave Hannah alone in the cold of a winter's day; she needed us to be with her. Yet I also didn't have any other words to say or feelings to express. Phil and I both felt emotionally depleted, and we clung to each other for the strength needed to walk away.

I glanced back several times for just one more look. The next time we would visit, the tent would be gone and a mound of dirt would be our only reminder of the time spent among a gathering of people, saying good-bye to Hannah Marie.

Samuel cried the entire ride from the cemetery to the church. My nerves were frazzled, and the emotions of the day only intensified his screaming. Once at the church, Patti took over again by feeding and changing him. After a long day with no nap, he finally fell asleep in the stroller.

The Lord restored our tired bodies, allowing us to enjoy the food and fellowship. The joy we felt at the funeral was still present, and it helped to keep our faith strong as we shared with those who talked to us during the meal. The reactions to Hannah's funeral were positive and encouraging. People were in awe of our strength and told us that the service was powerful and uplifting. Phil and I could not let an opportunity like that pass by without giving glory to God for His outpouring of grace. We wanted people to be convinced that God was to be praised for our reaction and not us!

We were so busy talking with other people and thanking them for coming that the time passed quickly. It was almost six o'clock when the tables were taken down and the floor swept. To those who had worked so hard to serve us, we blessed them with an arrangement of flowers to take home. The remaining flowers were delivered to our house by the funeral home later that evening.

We invited Norm, Janine, and their kids to come to our house and help us count the contributions that were donated in memory of Hannah. Since we didn't need any money to help pay for the funeral expenses, we decided that the funds should be spent on a missionary project centered on proclaiming the gospel to young children. (Approximately 4,000 dollars has been set aside for this cause. As of 2005, we are still praying and waiting on the Lord to show us how to best allocate the money.)

By 9 p.m. our house was empty—the earliest time that it had been vacated in days. We were exhausted from the day's events but didn't want to face the silence of our bed where thoughts about Hannah would surely come and cause pain. Phil's solution was to tune out in front of the TV by watching a movie. I stayed up with him for a little while, and when my eyes couldn't stay open a minute longer, went to bed and fell fast asleep, clinging tightly to Hannah's nightgown.

I have been told numerous times that this will be the hardest part about grieving: going back to normal life. I've discovered that it's actually not the hardest part so far—it's just different than before.

FEBRUARY 22, 2004
SANDY'S JOURNAL

People talk of the sacrifice I have made in spending so much of my life in Africa . . . It is emphatically no sacrifice. Say it rather a privilege. Anxiety, sickness, suffering, or danger, now and then, with a foregoing of the common conveniences and charities of this life, may make us pause, and cause the spirit to waver, and the soul to sink; but let this only be for a moment. All these are nothing when compared to the glory which shall be revealed in us. I never made a sacrifice.[1]

DAVID LIVINGSTON
MISSIONARY TO AFRICA

8

A Time to Heal

Sorrow is better than laughter, because a
sad face is good for the heart. The heart of
the wise is in the house of mourning . . . .

Ecclesiastes 7:3-4

IN THE DAYS FOLLOWING HANNAH'S FUNERAL, WE WERE
continually surrounded by our family and friends, at our request.
Being physically alone meant also being alone with our thoughts,
which at that time would have been too much to handle. The
distraction of children running through the house and adults chatting
about trivial things helped to keep ourselves from thinking about
Hannah every second.

Our telephone rang constantly. We received calls from
people who wanted to inquire about how we were doing and to say
they were praying for us. I don't think any of those who called
expected to find us in such high spirits. Cutting through the
background noise of what sounded like a party, we would yell into
the receiver, "Hey! What are you doing right now? Nothing, you
say? Great! Come on over and eat dinner with us! There's plenty
for everyone!"

Our invitation always left the friend who called, speechless:
"Well, um, OK! We'll be right over!" At one count there were
thirty people fellowshipping together in our modest-sized home. For
once I didn't feel overwhelmed by the chaos of people tripping over
each other and children trashing every room in the house!

Just as they had done before the funeral, Phil's mother and
Aunt Linda continued to serve almost every day in the kitchen. My

mother also joined them one afternoon to lend a hand. These gracious ladies rarely sat down to talk with our company but took greater joy in ministering to our family and guests instead. With quiet spirits they worked to glorify God, pouring their hearts into assisting our needs. Oh, how my mother-in-law's eyebrows would go up whenever she heard me on the telephone, inviting more friends to come share a meal with us! Yet I never heard her complain once about the extra work that would have to be done, or how we wouldn't have enough food. In fact, we often joked about how God miraculously provided, just as He had with the loaves and fishes.

In less than one week Phil and I suffered through many difficult things that most people will never experience in their lifetime: we held our daughter's lifeless body, planned a funeral, and buried one of our own flesh and blood. But no pain could be worse than going back to the cemetery the day after Hannah's burial.

When we had driven away from the cemetery the day before, the tent enclosed her spotless white casket, protecting it from the cold and wind of February. With this final picture in our minds, we were definitely unprepared for what we saw when visiting her grave.

The tent had been taken down, and a mound of dirt replaced the shelter it provided. The fresh flowers that had adorned Hannah's casket were sitting on top of the mound, already wilted. The snow and bitter wind whipped across the wide-open field with what seemed like a purposeful lack of sensitivity. *She's all alone,* we thought. *It feels so cold and desolate . . . and final.*

Nothing before this had stabbed my heart with greater pain. I imagined our daughter buried beneath the ground in a casket that was now stained with dirt. Although I knew Hannah couldn't feel anything, I had such a strong desire to dig up the dirt and cover her cold body with blankets. I wanted to protect and nurture my child but felt helpless and inhibited by the earth which separated us. The same soil that brought forth life and beauty in the spring now showed itself as an ugly covering for death, and I resented its betrayal.

I did not share these emotions with Phil, but I was certain he felt them as well. My husband lowered himself to one knee and caressed the dirt beneath him. I knelt down also, and we held each other tightly, crying uncontrollably. The sting of death had been felt by both of us for the first time since Hannah's death. Where was the joy and victory over the grave that we had sung about so often in our favorite hymns? This was the lowest point in my faith that I had ever experienced. The grave reminded me that Hannah's death was final; we would never see her again on this side of heaven. Suddenly, the life that God graciously extends to me seemed far too long to wait.

Valentine's Day came two days after the funeral on a Saturday. It was the first holiday spent without Hannah. Phil and I considered canceling our usual celebration, but for the sake of the children we decided to go ahead with the party and do our best to hide our true feelings. In keeping with our family tradition, Phil decorated the kitchen with all the fixings for a party: balloons, streamers, and small gifts for each of the children. When the kids made their way downstairs that morning, they were excited to see what Daddy had prepared for Valentine's Day. They were not disappointed.

It was difficult to sit around the festive table and see Hannah's chair, empty. Since her death, we had not dined alone as a family around the table. We could sense that even the children felt her absence as we ate our breakfast and opened gifts in silence.

The Valentine's Day celebration finished early, so we went to work cleaning up the house before company started to arrive. Being alone to our individual tasks left me feeling lost, and I had little motivation to accomplish anything productive. Finally, unable to tolerate the four walls of our house and the memories of Hannah within them, I decided to take a walk on our property. Perhaps I just needed to have a good cry in the crisp winter air where no one could hear me. It had been days since I had let it all out.

I wandered behind our house and walked among the pine trees. Once in a place where I was sure no one could see me, I knelt in the snow and prayed aloud with the only words I could think of: "Lord, I miss her. It hurts so much! Please, help me." I expected that being alone would trigger a flood of emotions, but no matter how hard I tried to cry, the tears wouldn't come.

Throughout the weeks and months following Hannah's death, I learned that crying was something I could not force myself to do or stop myself from doing. It was uncontrollable and unpredictable yet necessary in order to heal. I have come to believe this was God's grace upon me. What a mess I would have been if allowed to cry twenty-four hours a day!

During those moments of weeping it seemed as though God had temporarily removed His hand of protection from around my heart and allowed the hurt to enter in. Then, when spent of emotion, He would hold my heart again and help me to go on with life. There is no shame in crying, and God did not frown upon me for being sad. He knew my hurts and felt them with me. God was not cruel in the sense that He took Hannah away and then left us on our own to deal with it. *"Never will I leave you; never will I forsake you"* (Hebrews 13:5). A simple truth but so crucial to our survival through grief. I had never felt the Lord more near to me in all my life.

The guests cleared out of our home Sunday evening, and on Monday we were all alone as a family for the first time in a week. Monday afternoon, Phil's parents and Aunt Linda were scheduled to return to Florida to live for the remaining winter months. Grateful for all their help, we wanted to surprise them by showing up at the airport to see them off. In addition, a trip to the airport gave us a necessary focus for the day. The surprise was a success. They were blessed to be given one last opportunity to say good-bye, and I was thankful for being distracted from thinking of Hannah constantly.

It was hard knowing what to do next. Phil had been given an extended absence from work for as long as needed. With no motivation to live as "normal," we tried to think of ways to keep ourselves occupied. We considered loading up the family and driving down to Florida to enjoy the warm sunshine which would certainly lighten our heavy hearts. But thoughts of driving twenty-four hours with an eight-month-old baby and a discontent two year old caused us to quickly decide against it.

Then Phil started talking about leaving the children with friends and getting away alone. He reasoned that we needed to grieve together without the weight of caring for children, thereby strengthening our marriage and ultimately our family. I had mixed emotions about doing this. On the one hand, everything that reminded me about Hannah was at home, and I wanted to be near her. On the other hand, everything that reminded me about Hannah was at home, and this made me want to escape the sadness for a while to find some relief. In the end, I left the decision with Phil and trusted my loving leader to do what he felt was best for us.

Phil decided to use a gift certificate our next-door neighbors had given us for a night away at a newly-furnished hotel in downtown Kalamazoo, Michigan. Neither of us had ever spent time in that city, so we looked forward to checking it out.

The children went to stay with Matt and Helen Lowe for the four days that we would be gone. Our homeschool support group planned to provide all meals to the Lowe family while our children were in their care. This would help to ease the burden for Matt and Helen and also gave the group a way to help our family by helping theirs. Our children always enjoyed spending time at the Lowe's, and we had no reservations about leaving them behind. We were confident that Matt and Helen would provide sympathetic, loving care to our most precious possessions, who would not only be missing their mom and dad, but also their sister.

The hotel we stayed in was by far the nicest we've ever been to, and we thanked God for providing it through our kind neighbors. Phil and I spent the next three days in our exquisite suite, talking, crying, and reading the Scriptures together, along with a few other books about heaven and suffering. Being away from home and the children had lessened the intensity of our sorrow. It seemed as though Hannah was also at the Lowe's with her siblings, instead of living in heaven with Jesus. If the other children had come along with us, the hole left by Hannah would have been so obvious, and we could not have embraced what God was working in us through His Word.

God also used the hotel piano player to minister to our pain. One evening, while walking hand-in-hand through the lobby, we passed by the grand piano as it poured out rich, beautiful music. The black man seated at the keyboard called out to us in a soothing voice, "Ah, lovebirds! Can I play your song?"

Phil and I looked at each other and laughed. Little did this man know the trial that we had gone through just one week before. We strolled over to the piano and started talking to the "Piano Man," whose wrinkles and worn face made him look like he had been through a few trials of his own.

"You don't happen to know any hymns, do you?" asked Phil. At this question, the man's face unexpectedly lit up. "Ah, yes! Hymns are my favorite! What would you like to hear?"

For the next fifteen minutes, Phil and I stood around the piano singing our hearts out as the "Piano Man" played two of the hymns that were sung at Hannah's funeral and a few of his own favorite selections. We didn't care who walked by and saw us; in that moment it was just Phil, me, and the music in perfect harmony. Each day that we stayed at the hotel we went down to the lobby and listened to the heavenly music played by our new friend and, as we came to find out, our brother in the Lord. What an example of God's smiling providence!

Despite my initial hesitation, getting away alone was one of the best decisions we had made in our twelve years of marriage. God had answered the prayer that was spoken from our car on the morning of Hannah's death—this trial was not going to tear us apart. The retreat to Kalamazoo was the springboard God used to strengthen our marital bond through the tough year to come. We felt more prepared to face the trials that would test our faith and more certain that *"in all things God works for the good of those who love him, who have been called according to his purpose"* (Romans 8:28).

Our time away also taught us that God would take us through the grief process in different ways and hit us with the reality of Hannah's death at different times. When Phil was overcome with emotion, I stayed strong and calm, ready to comfort him. Likewise, during the times when I broke down in grief, Phil remained steady and prayed me through it. Neither of us had any expectations as to how the other should mourn. God gave us this revelation shortly after Hannah's death, and I believe that this kept our marriage together when many would have fallen apart under the same circumstances.

Once home again we had to face moving on without Hannah. Confronting each day was difficult because upon waking in the morning, the intensity of my pain felt the same as the night she had died. If it weren't for the other children, I would have been tempted to stay in bed all day. By getting up and having to serve their needs, the process of healthy grieving began almost immediately.

Two weeks after Hannah's death, I put some thoughts down on paper to help sort out my feelings. I wrote about how it felt to go back to normal life with a "hole" that had been dug by death:

> It's been two weeks since Hannah's death. This is the first day that I have felt the normalcy of living, and it is silently painful. Phil and I are fully parents again in sole charge of feeding, dressing, and disciplining the children. There is no one around to rescue us by taking over when we need to be alone. We are facing the "hole" head on but also learning to step around it. Sometimes I walk up to the edge and peer in as I am reminded of Hannah throughout the day. I linger there and think deeply about her, wishing she were sitting on my lap at church or taking her seat during our evening meal. But just when I feel that I might fall into the hole, the Lord gives me a happy remembrance of her, and I smile to myself. This gives me the strength to turn and walk away from the hole she has left in our lives. I go back to clearing the dinner table and telling Abigail for the third time, "Please sit down while you eat that cookie!"

It was essential for our lives to move forward, not only for the sake of our children but also as a testimony of God's faithfulness and to glorify His name. What kind of witnesses would we be to others, especially those who didn't know Christ, if we allowed the sadness to paralyze us?

If the shock of grief had kept us from moving forward, then we might not have seen how God was working. Even in our crippled condition of grief, God used our weakness to bring Himself glory, and we received joy in return. This was one of the lessons that suffering had taught us, almost from the very beginning. 1 Peter 4:13 says, *"But rejoice that you participate in the sufferings of Christ, so that you may be overjoyed when his glory is revealed."* This verse encourages us to rejoice when the trials come so that as we see God glorified by the impact of our suffering, abundant joy will result. (The joy I refer to is peaceful contentment, not feelings of light-hearted happiness.)

Having joy in the midst of suffering is a powerful instrument used to draw the world to Christ. Those who do not know the Savior should be able to recognize that we are Christians by our extraordinary joy. The Bible commands us, *"Consider it pure joy, my brothers whenever you face trials of many kinds, because you know that the testing of your faith develops perseverance"* (James 1:2-3). Being joyful instead of depressed was a daily *choice* Phil and I made in order to be obedient. It required the exercise of our own wills to express this joy. At times it was tempting to walk up to the line of depression and step over into the dark side. But during those moments, God spared us from this misery, helping us to turn away abruptly and not give in to our flesh. We chose to allow God to heal us in His way and in His time, without any "help" from us.

The verse in James continues on: *"Perseverance must finish its work so that you may be mature and complete, not lacking anything."* The trials that God brings us, great or small, are necessary in order for us to become more like Christ; we cannot be perfect and complete without them. God uses our suffering to strengthen our trust in Him and grow us in areas where we lack maturity. And for those who let the lessons of suffering be their teacher, the Scriptures promise a "crown of life": *"Blessed is the man who perseveres under trial, because when he has stood the test, he will receive the crown of life that God has promised to those who love him"* (James 1:12).

Pain has a purpose; it is for our good. Through suffering we grow in our faith, learn who God is, bring others to Christ, and in the end we receive a reward.

Isn't it interesting that following God comes easier for some than for others? Theology has an enormous amount to do with it. If you don't have a theological "place"—such as the sovereignty of God—to put your burden, then it's difficult to trust God enough to follow Him. There's no way to bring back a spouse who has died. There's no way to "un-drug" a son who's now in rehab. It's happened. The bad is there. Without a place to put the burden, you bear it alone. I think one's view of God is very, very, important . . . .

All things do work together for good. Knowing this is true, a person might say, "I'm not going to give up just because I have a son in rehab. Rather, I'm going to thank God that this problem was addressed, that my son is getting help. And, I don't know what the next turning point will be, but it has to be better than what it was going to be." That's why we can grieve with hope. We can endure sad times with joy.[2]

CHUCK SWINDOLL

❧❧

For the first few months after Hannah died, I could not get through a day without weeping. It was usually worse when alone at night while trying to fall asleep. My mind would scroll through the events surrounding Hannah's death, and it was difficult to turn off the images and surrender to sleep. Many nights I solved this problem by staying up until after midnight, becoming so tired that I fell asleep immediately upon hitting the pillow.

One night in particular, it was after midnight, but I was still having trouble going to sleep. Thoughts about my own growth as a Christian plagued my heart. It had only been less than a month since Hannah died, and I wanted so desperately to see the good that came from it. Were any lives truly changed for Christ and the kingdom? What about my own life? Many of the sins that I struggled with were slowly coming back: judgment and criticism of others, fretting over a perfectly clean house, materialism, discontentment, and impatience. I had thought these "thorns" could never possibly return as Hannah's death had forever impacted and changed me. As time progressed, however, I started to act like my sinful self again, and I hated it. "You haven't really changed!" spoke a voice inside my head. "In fact, no one has changed since Hannah died. It was all for nothing!"

I couldn't bear the thought that Hannah's death was in vain. I arose from my bed and went into the bathroom, grasping her nightgown in my hands. As soon as the door closed behind me, I buried my face in the nightgown and muffled my sobs so as not to wake anyone. "Lord, I miss her so much! Please, tell me You have a purpose in all this!"

God answered my prayer in a way I did not expect. In the midst of letting out my emotions, a picture of Hannah came to mind. Once again the vision of her running to Jesus was before me. But this time the image didn't end with Hannah jumping into His arms. The vision continued with Jesus holding Hannah closely as the two turned away and started walking toward heaven. I saw Hannah's smiling face peer over Jesus' shoulder as her tiny hand rose up to wave good-bye.

God's reply to my cry for help was to finish the vision He had given me earlier. He had allowed me to "see" how happy Hannah was as they entered into eternity together. It didn't matter what impact her death had on me, my family, or those who watched us. The real importance was to be found in the hope of the gospel! My daughter was with Christ, happier than she ever would be here on earth—no more sin, no more sickness, no more pain. Hannah does not want to come back and live with us, and honestly, Phil and I don't want her to. The pain that we must endure is worth experiencing for the sake of Hannah's joy and peace in heaven.

On the one-month anniversary of Hannah's death, Phil received an e-mail from Hannah's heart surgeon, Dr. Bove. He was responding to Phil's inquiry about the blood tests performed on Hannah while in the hospital. We had wondered if the bacteria which caused the infection, and ultimately her death, was ever found. While the answer to this question didn't plague us, we were slightly curious and hoped to have an answer.

Unfortunately, Dr. Bove's reply did not provide us with any conclusions. He stated that the infection might have been triggered by an undetectable virus. "I am shocked and stunned by Hannah's sudden death," he wrote. Although disappointed, I wasn't surprised. Hannah's birth, life, and now death had always been a mystery to doctors; we were used to news like this.

By this time the children and I were slowly easing back into our routine, and I became "Mom" again. There were still many basics that were lacking in our schedule, such as regular devotions, school, and chores. I became so focused on dealing with my own pain that my family didn't have the most sympathetic, loving mother at times. I often felt guilty for not taking better emotional and spiritual care of our children. But as my dear friends assured me,

"Your kids have learned so much from your response to Hannah's death. Take this time to heal and don't feel the pressure to go back to normal life so soon." Resting in this wisdom was hard to do, but I continued to trust that God would help restore our lives back to normal a little at a time.

Two questions that we were most often asked were: "How are you doing?" and "How are your kids handling this?" I knew how to answer for Phil and I, but wasn't always sure what to say regarding our children. Both Moriah and Nathan didn't speak much about their feelings, although I'm sure they were grieving, too. They saw us openly express our emotions, and we always gave them the freedom to do the same without shame. We also frequently talked and laughed about the funny things Hannah did, giving them an open door to talk about her in a way that wasn't always sad. Their behavior didn't show any outward signs of suppressed grief. In fact, they laughed, played, and argued with one another just as before.

We did our best to draw conversation out of our children, and at first their silence was alarming. We often wondered what more could be done to help them deal with their emotions. But finally it occurred to us that from the time Moriah and Nathan were very young, we had taught them that the things of the earth are not what we live for. We live and breathe to glorify God, knowing that one day, those who love Jesus will spend eternity with Him. Having heard this truth so often, they didn't know how else to think.

Nathan's comment one evening soon after Hannah's death assured me of this perspective: "Mom, I know that Hannah was born and died for a purpose." That settled it. Yes, both were sad and missed her, but they understood that this trial was all part of God's sovereign plan.

Abigail, on the other hand, was quite vocal about missing her sister. She often told me how much she wished Hannah would come back home: "Will she be home in the spring time?" I also overheard Abigail making up songs about her sister and best friend: "Hannah is in heaven now and I miss her . . . She's never coming back . . . She was my best friend and I want to play with her again . . . ." Abigail knew from what we told her that Hannah was in heaven with Jesus, but I doubt that she fully understood.

Abigail frequently expressed her disappointment, both verbally and physically, over not being able to play with Hannah. There was a solid three-month period of time when Abigail was anything but pleasant to be around. Tantrums and outright disobedience made for one unhappy little girl and two frustrated parents. It took us a while to figure out that the cause of Abigail's misbehavior might be a reaction to the sudden loss of her favorite playmate. Without compromising discipline when needed, we started to show her more love by thinking through our responses to her misbehavior with greater care and patience. By her third birthday in May, Abigail seemed to come out of her foul mood and was blossoming into the happy, comical child we once knew.

More than a year after Hannah's death, Abigail was still asking the same questions. We continued to explain that Hannah did not want to come back and live with our family because she was happier playing with other children in the presence of Jesus.

"Can I go to play with the other children, too?" she would ask.

"No, Abigail, not yet. Daddy and I want you to stay with us for now. But if you love Jesus, when you die you will go to heaven where Hannah is."

"Why did Hannah die? Was she sick?"

"Yes. She had a sick heart, remember?"

"Is she still sick in heaven?"

"No. Hannah is all better now. Jesus has healed her heart."

Not many children can recall the events that happen in their lives at so young an age, but I am hoping that Abigail will be an exception. She will always hear stories about her sister and see the pictures and videos, but I pray that her own memories of days spent with Hannah are immortalized in her mind forever.

The questions that Abigail asked did not reopen the wounds made by Hannah's death. Quite the opposite, I found answering her inquiries to be healing. I wished that others would have been more talkative about Hannah, but understandably, most didn't know what to say. They were afraid of saying something hurtful at the wrong time and place. I articulated my desire to talk more about Hannah with others in my journal:

Everyone else must move on with their lives, and even though I know they haven't forgotten yet, it seems like they are forcing us to move on by not talking about her. I don't have any expectations as to how others should act around us now that two weeks has passed; I know without a doubt that many fellow believers are continuing to pray for us. But part of me wants to go back to two weeks ago when we talked about Hannah in my crowded living room, remembering her life as a gift. Somehow those conversations kept her "alive."

As mentioned in my journal, Phil and I had absolutely no expectations on what others should have done to help care for us. As time passed, our family and friends became quieter but were not completely mute on the subject. Many cards and gifts were sent our way. Each day we looked forward to getting the mail for the encouragement we received from those letters. Our church family and homeschool support group provided meals for at least six weeks. What a blessing it was to not think about grocery shopping, meal planning, or preparation!

Many people repeatedly told us that they also missed Hannah and could not even fathom what we were going through. Those same people promised to pray for us, and I knew they were not expressing trite condolences. Several individuals volunteered to babysit our children so that I could quietly rest, get something done (such as writing this book), or go out with my husband on a date. Two women from our church even came over to pamper me with a manicure, pedicure, massage, and haircut!

Yet with all this support, there were still many times when I felt alone in my grief. I had several helpful conversations with my mother who had also lost a young daughter over thirty years before. But aside from her encouragement, I didn't know where else to turn with my thoughts and feelings.

A Christian support group for parents who lost children met together weekly in the Lansing area, but I was hesitant to attend. I felt as though the Lord wanted me to share my burdens solely with Him instead, looking to the Word for the encouragement I needed. (I am not saying that support groups in general are ungodly or unproductive. Rather, God was not leading me to be part of a such a group at that time.)

I also knew that my desire to join a support group stemmed from the wrong motives. Instead of going to encourage and be encouraged, I was expecting to impress them with my "strong" faith and belief that God is sovereign. How arrogant of me to think that I was in a better place than other grieving parents and could offer some assistance when not even a month had passed by!

Sometimes I tried too hard to make Hannah's death mean something. I quickly became weary of striving in my own efforts and broke down under the weight. God was the One who would bring glory to His name through Hannah's death according to His plan. Who was I to come up with my own strategy for how this should be accomplished?

If left to my own plan, the healing process would certainly not have included a pregnancy. Yet according to God's divine plan, that's just what happened. On March 28, the pregnancy test read positive—another Dufrin baby would be arriving in early December.

I am ashamed to confess that my feelings toward this child were not positive. How would I be able to cope with the changes of pregnancy and grieve for Hannah at the same time? Didn't God know that in the last six weeks I had expended all of my emotional energy, leaving nothing to help me handle a pregnancy?

In addition to these concerns, I was also embarrassed that others might consider me foolish for getting pregnant so soon. Was I trying to replace Hannah? When breaking the news I always followed with this explanation: "Well, this is not what I wanted, but obviously God thought differently." What a rejection of God's sovereignty and lack of trust in Him who had been so faithful to care for us! Many times I had to repent of my pride, asking God to forgive me for caring more about the opinion of others rather than rejoicing over the blessing of a new life. In my pregnancy journal, written to our baby, I talked about those feelings:

> God's timing is definitely strange, but I will continue to trust Him, knowing that He will sustain me throughout the next nine months. I believe wholeheartedly that children are a gift and blessing from God. The Bible says that they are a reward. We have been graciously rewarded with you! How I pray that I will find joy with this pregnancy in the midst of sorrow. Perhaps God has planned this to give us something else to think about other than Hannah.

Our family and friends will probably think that this has happened too soon after Hannah's death. Maybe they will think that we are trying to replace her. Believe me, there is no way to replace what we lost.

I feel the need to justify this pregnancy by saying this wasn't what I wanted and that God has unusual timing. I've had to go to Him several times and repent for this attitude and for rejecting His plan and sovereignty. Nine months is a long time away, and I know that I'll feel differently come December. It shouldn't matter what people think but only that my Lord and King is pleased with me!

Gradually we told our loved ones and, of course, most responded favorably. I was grateful for their encouraging reaction but was internally broken by the reality this new baby signified: life was moving forward and our family would never be the same. This child would grow up not knowing Hannah. There would be no pictures of Baby being held by his or her big sister. It was too soon after Hannah's death to face this, and at times I resented the pregnancy for this reason. How I prayed that God would change my heart as only He could!

Becoming pregnant intensified a dilemma that I never knew how to reckon. How should I answer those who asked, "How many children do you have?" Do I tell them that we have five children but not mention that one of them had died? Or should I be more bold and let everyone know that one of our children was now with Jesus? Perhaps to keep things simple I should not include Hannah at all and answer that we have four children. And now that I was pregnant, what answer should I give to those who asked, "How many children will this be for you?"

I found no easy answers to those questions. My responses included all those stated above, depending on my mood and who was asking the question. The real issue underlying all this confusion was again, my own pride. Before Hannah died I took great pleasure in notifying others that I was the mother of *five* children. Their shocked and sometimes horrified reaction fueled my conceit, and I put myself above them. God used the loss of Hannah to humble me. Instead of adding numbers to our family, we were going backwards and subtracting. It pains me to think that I considered raising four children less of an accomplishment than raising five.

In April, a letter arrived from the University of Michigan Hospital. On May 12, a memorial service was being held for those children who had died while being treated in their facility. Immediately my heart leapt inside, and I felt compelled to go.

Phil, on the other hand, had no desire to return to that place. I'm sure if I had told him how much it meant to me for him to attend, he would have come along. But honestly, I was neutral about his presence. This was one of those times when I gave Phil the freedom to grieve the way he wanted without being offended. For me, going back to the hospital where I had last seen Hannah alive was something I needed in order to heal. I called to tell the people in charge that I would be coming, alone.

Kristi agreed to babysit the children so that I could make the trip to Ann Arbor. While traveling on the highway I reminisced about the many journeys we made with Hannah to U of M in the past. I drove by the same Cracker Barrel restaurant where we had shared our last meal together before surgery. Driving into the parking structure caused me to recall the many frustrated occasions when I had been late for an appointment and could not find a convenient parking spot. Walking through the long hospital hallways took me back to the morning of surgery when Phil, Hannah, and I casually strolled together, holding hands and playing the "One, two, three!" game. I relived each moment over again on that afternoon in May, providing some closure and allowing a little more of my spirit the freedom to move on.

The service was surprisingly Christian in focus, although not perfect, as the name of Jesus was never mentioned. In order to include all faiths, I had expected the ceremony to be generic and somewhat New Age, but the songs and hymns all reflected faith in our God, and the pastors even read passages from the Bible.

Midway through the service, the parents were asked to bring forward a picture of their child along with a special memento. I had brought a black and white photo of Hannah and the Strawberry

Shortcake doll (that Moriah had taken quick possession of after Hannah died). For some reason, this part of the service was difficult for me. I glanced up at the table full of over thirty photos and suddenly started to cry without restraint. Emotions that I could not control rushed in all at once. All of the children who had died that year belonged to mothers who experienced similar feelings of grief. How many of them knew Christ and were trusting in His love and care to see them through? How could anyone go through the loss of a child without God?

The tears I cried reflected my thankfulness to the Lord and expressed the burden I felt for those who did not know Christ as their Savior. I was also deeply grieved over the loss of my own daughter and how hard it had been to live without her. Both Phil and I could attest that missing Hannah only seemed to get more difficult as time went on, not easier as everyone said it would. During her funeral, it had been only four days since we last spent time with Hannah, and so there hadn't been a chance to really miss her. But now, three months later, we felt her absence intensely and yearned to have her with us again.

At the conclusion of the service I looked around for someone to talk with, hoping to meet another mother who could relate to my feelings. A woman who sang in the choir saw me surveying the room and, seeing that I had come alone, decided to introduce herself. We talked for the next twenty minutes until most of the other people had left. While I appreciated her efforts to keep me company, I was disappointed that no connection had been made with another grieving mother. This was just another confirmation that God didn't want me to depend on anyone other than Him to help me through the pain. From that day forward I stopped trying to find my "grieving soul mate" and trusted that God would bring someone across my path if this was His will.

There was one more thing to do before leaving the hospital: take the elevator up to the Pediatric Intensive Care Unit on the fifth floor. I wanted to see the hallway where we paced, the telephone that we talked on, and the waiting room where we worried.

When the elevator doors opened I quickly stepped out and walked briskly to the door of the waiting room to scan it with my eyes. *There is the corner where Phil and I waited for the news of*

Hannah's surgery. Turning to the left I gazed at the double doors which entered into the unit. *Just beyond those doors is where the nurse told us that Hannah's heart had arrested.* Looking further to the left I noticed the pay phone on the wall and the chair underneath it. *We sat in that chair and made phone calls to our family with the news that Hannah was gone.* Then, before getting back on the elevator, I glanced at the nearby windowsill. *This is where Phil sat as we waited for the nurse to inform us about Hannah's status.* When the elevator doors flew open I swiftly stepped on and breathed a sigh of relief. I had done it; I had gone back to the place that held so many horrible memories for me. I successfully conquered the U of M monster, never letting that hospital disturb me again.

We marked the eighth day of every month as the anniversary of Hannah's death. "It's been four months since Hannah's been gone," we would say. It seemed that time was mocking us the further through the year we went. As the weeks and months passed by quickly, we were glad to be that much nearer to eternity, yet sad that our lives had adjusted without her. At the same time, the months seemed to crawl along slowly, and it felt as though it would be *an* eternity before seeing Hannah *in* eternity!

At the first sign of spring, Phil eagerly began work on a memorial garden in the middle of our backyard and visible from the kitchen where we spent most of our time as a family. Since Phil's mother has an extensive knowledge of plants, Phil asked her to go with him to the nursery to select the flowers that would be best.

After a full day of shopping, planning, and planting, the garden was complete. Each of the flowers they chose was reminiscent of Hannah's delicate, sweet spirit. A white wooden cross, painted with Hannah's name and bright flowers, was placed at the edge of the garden, telling the outside world for whom the garden was created.

When the weather warmed up and the children started to play outside more frequently, Phil and I enjoyed seeing them play near Hannah's garden. I cried many tears while doing dishes at the kitchen sink, watching through the window as the children played games among the flowers.

In April, a friend graciously offered to care for the children so that we could look for a monument to mark Hannah's grave. Not knowing where to go and having no recommendation from friends, we simply looked in the Yellow Pages and decided to browse at three different businesses.

The first we came to was closed in the middle of the day due to a death in the family. We would have passed right by the second location if it weren't for the sign that read, "Serving the Lansing area for fifty years." The place itself was small and visually unimpressive from the outside, but the longevity of service and the caring assistance convinced us to stay. An instant connection was made with the elderly shop owner who, after meeting us said, "Choosing a monument is a very personal thing. You'll want something that reminds you of the good memories with your daughter, something that tells who she was just by looking at it." Phil and I knew we need shop no further.

Not one of the designs offered for children spoke "Hannah" to us. There were plenty of angels, lambs, and baby images to choose from, but all those seemed too plain and ordinary. After spending over an hour looking at options and feeling discouraged, the saleswoman asked, "Have you ever considered putting Hannah's picture on the monument?"

When first browsing the showroom, I had looked at the examples of monuments with photographs mounted on them but didn't think this was appropriate for Hannah. But when considered a second time, the idea took root in my mind. I could envision our family visiting the cemetery and "talking to Hannah" while looking at her picture. Rather than thinking about her lifeless body in the ground, we could dwell on the peacefulness of her face and sweetness of her smile instead.

My thoughts were confirmed by Phil, and we began creating a design that included a photograph taken from our family picture just one week before Hannah died. We chose to have flowers etched around the oval picture with ribbons flowing from them to represent the ribbons that I often tied in her hair. The monument we selected was small, and there wasn't much room on the front for anything more than Hannah's full name, date of birth, and date of death. Beneath these inscriptions we also included an epitaph—"Safe in the arms of Jesus"—a reminder of the vision of Hannah running into Jesus' arms and being embraced by Him. The design was simple but perfectly represented who Hannah was in her four years of life.

In June, when Phil and I saw the finished monument at the cemetery for the first time, neither of us could stop staring at her name engraved permanently in bold black letters: HANNAH MARIE DUFRIN. "That's *our* name in the granite," Phil said. "I don't know how to feel about seeing our last name on a grave marker."

Tears instantly came to my eyes. Like Phil, I was also experiencing a confusing mix of emotions. Finally, after four long months of waiting, Hannah's grave was properly marked, and we now had something physical to visit and talk to. I couldn't have been happier about the way the monument turned out. But my spirit was crushed at the finality that the marker symbolized. This was one more confirmation that Hannah was indeed gone. This was *not* just a dream—Hannah was *dead*. How I hated thinking of her in that way!

Feeling the cold, hard granite had caused me to reflect on her death in cold, hard terms. These feelings were similar to the day when we visited Hannah's grave site for the first time after the funeral. At that time I had falsely concluded there was nothing glorious or beautiful about death. The cemetery had become a place where I found no comfort or peace for my sorrows. This was not the way I wanted to think, as we planned on visiting there with the children many times throughout the summer months. Perhaps adding signs of life to Hannah's grave would help me to view the cemetery more positively.

We began work during the first week of July on a small garden that would surround Hannah's monument. Our homeschool support group had given us a gift certificate to a garden nursery where we could buy a tree in remembrance of Hannah. Our neighbor, who owned a small tree farm, also offered to donate a tree in Hannah's memory. So rather than having two trees planted in our yard, we decided to use the gift certificate to purchase materials needed for the cemetery instead.

It had been almost two hours before we left the nursery in our van loaded with perennial plants. The nursery worker was extremely valuable in helping us to select flowers that would survive in sandy soil, under the direct sun, and with little water.

Once back at the cemetery, we employed the children's help to create Hannah's garden. Phil plowed the ugly soil, and I dug holes for the plants. We placed a plastic border around the garden to close it in and added wood chips. The children hauled away the dirt and watered the flowers after planting. When finished, we stood back with our arms around each other, admiring our work and smiling with pleasure. Already the monument seemed softer because of the life the tender flowers displayed.

Tending to Hannah's grave site gave our family a good reason to visit the cemetery, bringing me the joy and peace I needed. My desire to nurture Hannah was fulfilled every time we weeded, watered the plants, and filled the bird feeder. The children, especially Moriah, regularly asked if we could go "visit Hannah," and we complied with their request even if inconvenient. Abigail gave the cemetery a new name, calling it "Hannah's Park." To her, there was nothing sad or depressing about going there; it was simply a place to run, laugh, and play!

Watching our children scamper among the grave markers while laughing with delight has helped put Hannah's death into proper perspective. Our children undoubtedly miss their sister, but their loss is softened by the realization that earth is not our real home. *"But our citizenship is in heaven. And we eagerly await a Savior from there, the Lord Jesus Christ . . ."* (Philippians 3:20). I am thankful to God that Hannah's brothers and sisters have a healthy view of death which will carry them through the trials of life. God's plan may be that one of them will also be called to suffer for His sake. Observing our response to Hannah's death may help them not hesitate to trust Christ if their lives should take a similar turn.

I'm certain that our family was most remembered and prayed for during the times when families gathered to celebrate special events and holidays. We were often asked how we made it through those days without falling apart. I wondered about this myself and looked toward those celebrations with dread. But as time went on, we learned that living without Hannah in the routine of everyday life was much more difficult than during the holiday seasons. Perhaps this was due to the number of people whom the Holy Spirit prompted to pray for us when we needed His mercy the most. In answer to those prayers, God's grace was abundantly supplied, covering our family and allowing us to get through those occasions with peace.

Hannah's birthday came six months after her death on August 2. Phil had taken the day off of work so that I wouldn't be alone with the children while trying to deal with my emotions. Without any formal plans until the evening, we carried on throughout the day as normally as possible, doing whatever helped to ease the pain.

Phil and I decided that Hannah's birthday was a fitting time to finally remove her hospital bag from our bedroom closet and unpack the clothes and toys. Wanting a permanent place to store her belongings, Phil had purchased a wicker-covered wooden trunk for this purpose and gave it to me as a gift for our 13th wedding anniversary in July. Alone in our bedroom, we knelt together in front of the trunk, and with tears streaming down our faces, carefully arranged the funeral mementos, greeting cards, Hannah's clothing, favorite game and book, hair ties, sippy cup, and "Blankie." Another chapter of Hannah's life, closed; another hurdle in our grief, crossed.

Up until that point we had not watched any home videos of Hannah. I don't think many understood why we weren't aching to see her walking and talking again. My heart did indeed long to see her on the screen, but I also knew that a rush of painful emotions would enter my heart, and I wanted to avoid them. "Which day should I chose to be sad?" I had explained to one friend. Most of the time we got through the days well, with periods of grief here and there. This in itself was enough to handle—the sorrow of seeing all that we were missing might have been too much.

However, because of Hannah's birthday, we thought it was time to let our guard down and watch the videos. One portion of the video in particular left me stunned, and I sobbed uncontrollably.

Routinely before bedtime, Phil had always read poems to Hannah and Abigail from a children's book entitled *Jesus Loves Me.* He read to them so often that they had come to memorize many of the verses. On video, Phil asked Hannah to recite the poem "Friend of the Little Children." These were the last words she would speak in front of the camera before her death.

> Jesus, friend of the little children,
> Be a friend to me.
> Take my hand and ever keep me
> Close to Thee.
>
> Teach me how to grow in goodness
> Daily, as I grow.
> Thou hast been a child,
> And surely Thou dost know.
>
> Never leave me nor forsake me,
> Ever be my friend,
> For I need Thee from life's dawning
> To its end.

Jesus was indeed Hannah's friend. Like the vision God gave me upon her death, this was confirmation that Hannah was "close to Thee" in the presence of Christ.

On the afternoon of Hannah's birthday we went to the cemetery as a family to spend some needed time alone. Our children brought Hannah a bouquet of helium balloons and tied them to the stake which held the bird feeder. It was an emotional time as we stared at her grave and pondered the cake that would never be made, the gifts that would never be given, and the "Happy Birthday" song that would not be sung. Yet in the midst of the emotional void those memories gave us, the hope and joy of Christ shone through, causing us to rejoice. Hannah's birthday was not only a time to remember her life, but also an occasion to savor the promises of Him who died for us.

Later that evening, we shared the day with others by inviting several families to meet us at the cemetery. Phil and I took great pleasure in showing our friends the monument and garden. After a time of talking, laughing, and reminiscing about Hannah, we gathered around her grave and sang "How Great Thou Art." As our voices soared together in harmony, the storm clouds that had been rolling in culminated in a clap of thunder. The words of the hymn synchronized beautifully with the wonder of God's creation: "I see the stars; I hear the rolling thunder; thy power throughout the universe displayed." Suddenly, my focus was not on Hannah or the suffering we had endured; it was fully on God. Yes, the Creator of the universe and all that is within was still in complete control. Nothing took Him by surprise. Hannah's death and our pain was all part of His sovereign plan.

When I consider how big God is and how long eternity will be, our plight seems small in comparison. And when I think about how awesome God is, I am also humbled by the depth and width of His *love* for me, a small, insignificant person. *"And I pray that you, being rooted and established in love, may have power, together with all the saints, to grasp how wide and long and high and deep is the love of Christ . . ."* (Ephesians 3:17-18). The Giver of Gifts blessed me on Hannah's birthday with the best present of all: the realization of how much He really loves and cares for me.

My heart overflowed with joy as we ran from the grave site to escape the pouring rain. Now I was truly in the mood to celebrate! Our friends had invited everyone back to their home where dinner was waiting. They wanted to share Hannah's birthday with us but didn't want Phil or I to be concerned about hosting company at our house. I was so grateful to them for showing care to our family in this way.

A few weeks prior to Hannah's birthday I had prayed that God would show me a creative way to remember her life. My gracious Lord heard that prayer and answered faithfully. Since the library in our little town of Williamston had a limited amount of children's books to choose from, I wanted to help enlarge their collection. So I sent letters to our family members and church friends, asking them to donate a book to the library in memory of Hannah. I also requested that the books be wrapped in paper and delivered to us before her birthday so that we could open them together as a family.

The idea was a success, and almost everyone we wrote to responded with enthusiasm. Our own children also participated by shopping with me at the local bookstore. Each child, including little Samuel, chose a book they knew Hannah would have enjoyed.

I had expected each family to contribute just one book for a total of approximately twenty titles. Having experienced their generosity so recently, I should not have been surprised when sixty-two books were donated! There were several books about princesses (appropriate for a daughter of the King!), and a multitude of books about Strawberry Shortcake, ballerinas, Cinderella, heaven, and loss. Opening the gifts brought us so much happiness as we delighted in the choices people made with Hannah in mind. It was a perfect end to the first birthday spent without Hannah. And the birthday girl herself was, no doubt, celebrating the glory of Christ with us from her eternal home in heaven.

SPENT APART
Written to Hannah for her fifth birthday by Daddy

Though months have passed and life has changed
My thoughts still drift to you.
That joyful smile,
Your warm embrace,
A voice that will not be erased.
Oh, how I've wished it were not true.

This day which would have been your fifth
From birth you saw but four.
Cakes and gifts,
Songs sung by all,
Laughter and joy I still recall.
I long to see you here once more.

I wake to thoughts that bring despair
And question why you've gone.
A failed attempt,
A different day,
Perhaps if we had just delayed.
All hope and trust appear withdrawn.

But He who holds you now with care
Is One who will not fail.
His grace complete,
His knowledge sure,
I know that I am held secure.
This lack of faith will not prevail.

Please question not why strength seems gone
Or where is Daddy's heart.
Christ is my King,
I shall not turn,
It is again for me to learn.
Another day so spent apart.

¤¤¤

Losing our daughter to death has peaked my interest in heaven more than ever before. Most of my questions center on Hannah and what she is doing there: Will she always remain four years old? Is another mother taking care of my little girl until I arrive? With whom has she made friends? Does God allow her to see glimpses of what goes on down here on earth? Has He told her the future? After searching the Scriptures for answers, much of what heaven is like still remains a mystery. Even so, I've never longed for it more. Hannah will be there waiting at the gate to welcome me and to give me a tour of the mansion. But even more glorious, standing alongside of her will be my Lord and Savior, Jesus Christ, the One who paid all my debts and gave me eternal life by His grace alone. What more about heaven do I need to know than this?

Hannah does not miss her earthly life. From her perspective, time does not move slowly in heaven as she waits for Phil, me, and the children to join her. As the holidays come and go and new family memories are made, I've gained peace knowing that Hannah hasn't missed out on anything. The joy of fellowshipping together as a family cannot compare to the ecstasy she experiences in the presence of Christ. Sometimes I imagine Hannah peering down from heaven to humorously reprimand me for my selfishness in wanting her back: "Mama, don't be sad. I love it here! See you soon!" Oh, how this thought has helped me through many rough times!

More and more I am thankful that Hannah is with God instead of suffering with the sin of this life. The beauty of our earthly experience pales in comparison to what she sees every day in heaven.

When autumn arrived and Hannah wasn't there to go apple picking with us, I took comfort in knowing that the fruit trees in heaven offer more delicious apples. Hannah can help herself to them at any time.

When the bright orange pumpkins grew in our garden and we brought them to "show" Hannah, I rested in knowing that the colors of heaven are so much more vibrant and beautiful.

When we sat together as a family next to Hannah's grave, eating donuts and cider on a warm fall day, I remembered that the weather in heaven is perfect every day.

When Christmas morning arrived and Hannah wasn't there to open her presents, I took joy in knowing that the best gift of all, Jesus Christ, dwells with her in heaven. She doesn't need anything else in order to be happy. And neither do we.

The well-known verse in Scripture that I most often quoted after Hannah's death is found in Job: *"The Lord gave and the Lord has taken away; blessed be the name of the Lord."* When thinking about how we were able to stand firm in Christ through this trial, I can echo Job's words. But for me personally, this verse has a more literal meaning than how Job intended it. In the course of one year, the Lord chose to take Hannah away and ten months later blessed us with another child—a son. On December 1, 2004, Aaron Peter

Dufrin made his quick entrance into the world; a little bit of heaven opened up as we received him from God.

All throughout my pregnancy I had hoped we would have another daughter—a little girl with big brown eyes and long, wavy hair. Although I realized there was no way to replace Hannah, I wanted some part of this child to resemble her. Deep down, my desire was that our family go back to the way it was before: two sons and three daughters. Somehow I thought Hannah's absence wouldn't seem so obvious if there were another girl to fill the hole she had created.

All the physical signs of pregnancy pointed to having a girl, and I was sure that God was going to fulfill my heart's desire. My friends wisely cautioned me to prepare my emotions for the arrival of a son. They were concerned that I was trying to make a substitute for Hannah and, if to us a son was given, that I might fall into depression. As the nine months drew to a close, I still held on to the hope for a daughter but was willing to accept whatever God had planned for our family.

I will always wonder if Hannah was told by Jesus that she would have another brother. I can imagine her laughter as Phil exclaimed with astonishment in the delivery room, "It's a boy?!" For only three seconds did I feel disappointed with this outcome. God's grace was upon me once again as I cried tears of joy rather than tears of remorse that another prayer was not answered the way I wanted. Yet another opportunity to learn that God is in control, and He plans all things for our good.

Bringing another child into our home was a difficult transition for us. Aaron's birth symbolized that our lives had physically moved forward without Hannah. We were a family of seven again, but the dynamics would not be the same. Phil and I felt the bittersweet emotions of both loss and joy. We were sad over what could have been, yet happy to have been given another child to raise. A woman's emotions are not always rational following a birth, so I tried to keep this in perspective. Even so, I missed Hannah so much and cried often as I looked into the face of my newborn baby. Those feelings kept our love for Aaron at a distance during his first days, and we relied on God once more to help us through.

Our dear friends in Christ sympathized with our pain and prayed for us during this time. God faithfully answered those petitions by removing the bitterness, allowing joy to take over in our hearts. Slowly I began warming up to our new baby, and love for little Aaron grew.

Aaron's name in Hebrew means "giver of light." We chose this name because having a new baby was a definite bright spot in our year of darkness. Aaron has truly lived up to his name as the most happy child of our six. While he does not resemble Hannah's physical features in the way I had hoped, Aaron did inherit her sweet, content disposition. His smile lights up a room, and that is no exaggeration! I cannot imagine our lives without him. God knew exactly what we needed and when we needed it. I am so thankful that He gave Aaron to us so soon after Hannah's death. His presence has played an instrumental role in healing our family.

As the year turned from 2004 to 2005, something changed within me. It felt as though a cloud had lifted, and I was more myself. My ability to pray wholeheartedly returned, and that part of my heart which kept me unmotivated in certain areas was finally relinquished to God. All of the firsts that we needed to get through without Hannah—vacations, holidays, her birthday—were complete, and as the months continued to pass by, the pain had lessened. Our family was moving on and peace was found within.

In the weeks leading up to the first anniversary of Hannah's death, I was driven to finish the manuscript for this book. There were many nights when I had stayed up until one or two o'clock in the morning to write from the darkness of my bedroom where Phil was sleeping. It was important for me to complete Hannah's story before the first anniversary because I had planned on giving a copy of it to Phil as a gift.

It was Carmen's idea to babysit the children the weekend before February 8 so that Phil and I could return to the Radisson in Kalamazoo. At first it sounded like the perfect plan, but I struggled over the cost of lodging at this very expensive hotel. In many ways it would be so meaningful to stay in the same place where the Lord had ministered healing to us one year before. But as worthy a reason as this was, I still had a hard time justifying the expenditure of so much money!

I had made a reservation with the hotel but was not fully convinced this was the right thing to do. Then, the night before we were to leave, Janine unexpectantly arrived at my back door, handed me an envelope, and abruptly walked away before I could respond.

"What is this all about," I said to myself out loud. I tore open the envelope and pulled out the card that was inside. A large sum of cash bills slipped from the bottom as I opened the card. It read:

> Dear Phil and Sandy,
>   We just wanted you to know that we're thinking of you and Hannah at this time. We're praying for you. Enjoy yourselves this weekend as you remember your darling girl. May this gift from all of us help you to that end.
> >   God's Peace!
> >   Covenant Life Community Church

The people of our church, who knew of my indecision, had taken up a collection to help offset the price of the room! Unlike me, they were confident that the best place to help us remember Hannah's life was back in Kalamazoo, no matter what the cost. Immediately I started to cry at their display of kindness. I called Phil at work and was so emotional over this provision that I could barely tell him the news. No more fretting or worrying—Friday, February 4, we were off to Kalamazoo!

Once settled into our room, I presented Phil with a spiral-bound copy of Hannah's story, and we spent two days reading it aloud together. Through the laughter, joy, heartache, and tears we reminisced about Hannah's life and were astonished at all the ways God had been faithful during her surgery, death, and through the grief which followed.

I'm not sure which period of time spent in Kalamazoo was more difficult—one *week* or one *year* following Hannah's death. Phil in particular struggled more with his emotions during our second stay. Many of the forgotten events and feelings I chronicled in Hannah's story were brought to the surface, forcing Phil to deal with them all at once. Reading the book together did not affect me quite the same way as it did Phil. I had written Hannah's story over the course of one year and was able to process the memories a little at a time. Our weekend away did give us a necessary break from life for a while, but the roller coaster of emotions kept us from truly enjoying one another's company.

On Sunday, February 6, exactly fifty-two weeks after Hannah died, our church held a special service to glorify God for what He had done as a result of Hannah's death. I was so thankful for Norm's thoughtfulness in planning this service and even more thankful that the focus was not to praise Hannah or our family but to give glory to God. We looked forward to hearing all the ways that the Lord had used Hannah's life and death to accomplish His purpose.

Although the songs we sang were the same as those from one year before, my heart in worshipping Christ was in a totally different place. Many of the things I learned about God because of Hannah's death could not have been gained any other way. The *joy* that overflowed as a result of knowing Him deeper had replaced the overwhelming shock and pain. The tears I cried were not ones of anguish or sorrow, but were expressions of the *peace* that I did not think was possible to have in a trial like ours. I raised my hands while singing to God, not in surrender to His frowning providence, but rather to embrace His *loving* will for my life. There was no other time in all my life when I worshipped God with my heart so focused on Him.

After Norm preached a short sermon from James 4, the floor opened up for people to come forward and give their testimony. Phil was the first to speak. How do you encapsulate the overwhelming faithfulness of God in such a short amount of time? Phil began by sharing an observation he made while eating dinner during our recent trip to Kalamazoo:

We were in a restaurant—it was a buffet—and Sandy went up and I stayed with Aaron. I watched this guy come from the parking lot. He was a big guy, and he walked as if his family—a wife and daughter—wasn't even with him. They all went to the table and sat down. Then he went up without them to get his own food, and I just watched him because I had this time to sit. I continued to watch them through the meal, glancing over at them. It was like he didn't care; he didn't care that he had a little girl.

My heart—my stupid, depraved heart (which is probably what I've learned most this year)—went to saying, "God, why did you take mine? Why didn't you take his? He doesn't care!" I didn't go too far with this. It wasn't as if I was angry and raising my fist—it was just a quick thought.

I forget at what point [during the weekend] when Sandy said to me, "Have you ever read Psalm 73?" I want to read it to you. Don't think this cruel or harsh.

> *Surely God is good to Israel,*
> *to those who are pure in heart.*
> *But as for me, my feet had almost slipped;*
> *I had nearly lost my foothold.*
> *For I envied the arrogant when I saw*
> *the prosperity of the wicked.*
> *They have no struggles;*
> *their bodies are healthy and strong.*
> *They are free from the burdens common to man;*
> *they are not plagued by human ills.*
> *Therefore pride is their necklace;*
> *they clothe themselves with violence.*
> *From their callous hearts comes iniquity;*
> *the evil conceits of their minds know no limits.*
> *They scoff, and speak with malice;*
> *in their arrogance they threaten oppression.*
> *Their mouths lay claim to heaven,*
> *and their tongues take possession of the earth.*
> *Therefore their people turn to them*
> *and drink up waters of abundance.*
> *They say, "How can God know?*
> *Does the Most High have knowledge?"*
> *This is what the wicked are like—*
> *always carefree, they increase in wealth.*
> *Surely in vain have I kept my heart pure;*
> *in vain have I washed my hands in innocence.*
> *All day long I have been plagued;*
> *I have been punished every morning.*
> *If I had said, "I will speak thus,"*

I would have betrayed your children.
When I tried to understand all this,
it was oppressive to me
till I entered the sanctuary of God;
then I understood their final destiny.

"Till I entered the sanctuary of God; then I understood their final destiny." This is not to say that I am pleased with their end or of this man's end or anything like that. I don't find pleasure in that—please don't mistake me.

I have learned this year how precious God's Word is to me. When I picture coming into this sanctuary, it all melts away. When I come and picture your faces—the people of God—the questions disappear and my gratitude is great. And so I thank all of you, and more than you, I thank God for what He's done through you for my family. You have blessed us more than I can ever repay you. I pray for opportunities to pay you back. I'm not praying for calamity to come, but we look for ways to bless those who have blessed us. I am thankful for this body; I am so thankful to God. And more than anything I am thankful for this—the Bible. I would be very mistaken if I did not thank God for that.

For the next hour, many other people stepped into the pulpit and summarized how God used Hannah's death to change their hearts and draw themselves closer to Him. I've included several short excerpts from those testimonies in order to reveal some of the good that came from losing our daughter.

I've looked at my children now with this idea of brevity—the briefness of life. I've looked at my children in a different light. I've stopped to actually look at their faces, to enjoy the sound of their voice a little bit more this year.

I think the thing that this last year has brought home to me since Hannah's passing is a deeper appreciation for the sovereignty of God and His kindness, and how He's been merciful to my family. That may seem strange to some people, especially in the light of

Hannah's passing. But she's in a better place. We have the Lord to lean on as a family, and He *has* comforted us.

It took a long time, but not too long ago—verbally, out loud, in front of my wife—I accepted Christ as my Savior. It was a life-changing experience for me . . . .

To Phil and Sandy: God truly blessed us with you two, and the way you have handled this has inspired me. It has gotten me through a lot of tough times . . . I just wanted to thank you guys and to thank God for giving you the strength and faith to get through this. Hannah was truly, in a very unique way, a blessing for Stormy and I, and certainly for Mason.

We'll probably never know the extent of how her life and death really impacted everybody, but one thing I can tell for sure: God used that in our children's lives to teach them about Himself. [Our daughter] Vika, accepted Christ shortly afterwards. He did not depend on Hannah to teach her of that, but He chose that as an awakening time for her.

A couple things I've learned this year that I believe God taught me through Hannah's death is to count the things of this world as rubbish. I had gotten into a laziness in my Christian walk; God's going to grow me in His time and in His way, and I'm going to rest and wait. Philippians says that's wrong: "Work out your salvation." So I've worked a little bit harder this year. He will grow me—sanctification is all for His glory, but I need to work, too. And I want to work; I want to grow. So I praise Him for that. It's been a good year.

And the second thing is: It's caused so much talk of heaven with my children. Each one has said to me this past year, "We're not afraid to die, Mom. Our bodies die, but our spirits live forever!" They get it! They're excited to go. And I praise Him for that. I think without Hannah dying I would have avoided the whole topic of death with my children. But you can't when their friend goes.

I'm excited to go to heaven; I'm excited to see her. I can say I'm not as afraid with what God has for our family because I know that He is going to get us through it. I've seen that first hand.

God is using sweet little Hannah in our lives. This life is but a mist. I don't want to live for this world anymore. I don't want to live for what pagans choose to do—we've spent enough time doing that. Let's live for the will of God and be radical! Let's not waste our life!

Throughout Hannah's life, God has been bringing us closer to a deeper understanding of His sovereignty. He taught us so many things about His ultimate control, and, as we learned from R.C. Sproul, there is not a random molecule outside of the power of God. There is something to having that head knowledge, and then there is living it out. It is obvious to me that He was grounding us in this teaching to prepare us for this time so that we could say, "The Lord gives and the Lord takes away—blessed be the name of the Lord!"

After the shock, there was a period of dark grief for me, and I would say a time of doubting that God really cared about us. There were some times of anger for me too, as I felt hopeless and wondered what the point of anything was. I had no desire to read the Bible, and I felt pretty much numb to everyone and everything.

The incredible changes that began to occur came through my husband. Between what happened with Hannah and some other things, it was awesome to see him take more interest in the things of God. Having the Word read aloud in our home and having his desires change, it changed my heart, which had grown cold in many ways. I have seen the living God at work.

I am learning to trust in God in new ways, and my views of Him have changed for the better. His Word is becoming more precious to me, and I am learning to discern between truth and emotion. I am learning to judge less and scrutinize more, and my heart continues to long to be soft instead of hard.

When it appeared that everyone had been given an opportunity to speak, I decided to close the service by sharing how God had used Hannah's death to raise my affections for Him:

I had commented at Hannah's funeral that—I think the very last thing I said was—may her death not be in vain. And listening to all of your testimonies today just encourages my heart so much to know that it wasn't. There is good in it, and God has shown us that through this year.

Daren, hearing you give your testimony about coming to Christ was probably the most gloriously satisfying thing I could hear today! God used Hannah as one means to bring you into the kingdom.

I am in more love with God now than I have ever been in my life, and I honestly would not trade it to have her back. She doesn't want to come back here, anyway. I picture her looking down from glory, chastising me: "Mama, don't be sad. I'm happy here!" Isn't that where we all want our children to be? The love I feel for God is so worth not having her here, and the joy I feel is so abundant—I only have Christ to thank for that. So much of what I have gone through this year has brought me so close to Him, and there is a joy in suffering. The irony of it is, I wish you could all have that joy, but I don't want you to have it in the way I experienced it.

I'm so thankful to all of you. I know that you've been praying for us so sincerely and genuinely. The grace that God has given is just unbelievable. It is only by His grace that we are where we are today and can stand and praise God for what He has done. Thank you so much. There is no other body of people that we'd rather belong to than this group here. Small as we are, our faith in God is not small, and your devotion to God is huge. I would not want to go anywhere else.

I know that you loved her and miss her almost as much as I do. I don't fear death—I cannot wait to get there, not just because she's there, but because Christ will be next to her. And it's only because of Him that I will see her again, and that love I have for Him is just . . . I can't even talk about it. Thank you.

On February 8, 2005, the first anniversary of Hannah's death, Phil had taken the day off from work so that we could spend time together as a family. That morning I was stirred from my sleep by the aroma of freshly-baked biscuits—this had been Hannah's favorite breakfast.

Phil had woken up early and, after thoughts of Hannah kept him from falling back asleep, decided to get a head start on the day. I could hear the quiet voices of the other children conversing with him downstairs in the kitchen. Since everyone was already awake except for Aaron and me, I decided to get out of bed too, even though my weary body could have slept an hour or more longer. It had been quite an emotional week leading up to this day, and the exhaustion had finally caught up with me.

After a grueling few days in Kalamazoo, followed by the high of an uplifting church service on Sunday, I hoped that the emotions for the day would fall somewhere in between. We had decided to approach this anniversary somewhat relaxed and informally so that there would be time to reflect on the past year without the demands of a schedule. Watching Hannah's videos consumed many hours, and while this caused a swing of emotions from joy to sorrow, we found great solace in seeing her again.

Amid the videos and duties of cooking and caring for the children, I ran out to the printer's shop in order to make several copies of my manuscript. On the way home I stopped by the cemetery to "show" Hannah the book I had written about her life. "Look, Hannah," I said through the tears. "I finally finished it. This is your story. I pray that your life will continue to reach people for Christ long after you are gone."

When I arrived home, it was Phil's turn to visit the cemetery. Originally we had wanted to go as a family, but both Moriah and

Nathan had come down with fevers that afternoon, and we didn't think it was wise to take them outdoors. Phil looked a little more worn upon returning home. But since the dinner hour was fast approaching and company would soon be arriving, there wasn't much time for him to dwell on it. Preparing food and cleaning the house became welcomed distractions.

We invited the same group of friends who had helped us to remember Hannah's birthday back in August. I looked forward to their company, and our hearts were light as we fellowshipped together over Hannah's favorite meal—nachos. Following dinner, everyone moved into the living room where we watched a video of Hannah. The conversation continued with questions about how Phil and I felt about the day, and we recalled the events that took place one year before.

In the midst of the discussion I snuck upstairs and gathered together the copies of this book, which were tied closed with a pink satin ribbon. Because our dear friends had been so much a part of our testimony, I wanted them to be the first people to read Hannah's story. It was my gift to them for praying us through the grief and for supporting our family so faithfully.

The evening ended in the most God-glorifying manner imaginable as we gathered around the piano and sang praises to the Lord. When nine o'clock rolled around, no one wanted to leave; the Spirit's presence made us feel so joyful inside. But since it was the middle of the week and babysitters needed to be relieved at home, the house had cleared out by 10 p.m.

Phil and I retired to the bedroom and compared the day's events to those of one year before. A lot had changed. Hannah was gone; a piece of our hearts had died; God supplied His grace through the suffering; our love for Him filled the void; and Aaron became part of our family. But perhaps the biggest change of all was evidenced by our faith in God: our love for Him was deeper; our belief in His sovereignty was stronger; and our trust in His plan was greater. While at one time I doubted whether Hannah's death had really impacted me, I finally reached a conclusion: Yes, I *was* different now, and the changes that Hannah's death brought about were indeed good for me.

Thank you, God for giving us Hannah; she was a blessing we did not deserve. I also thank you for taking her away. This, too, was a blessing, as there would have been no other way to grow deeper in love with You apart from losing her.

I cannot wait to hold my little girl again . . . . See you soon, Hannah! What a glorious day it will be!

The "intense joy" comes from the sense that you endured with the help of Christ. You have been proven in the fire and you have come through as genuine. You did not recant. Christ is real in your life. He is for you the all-satisfying God that He claims to be.[3]

If we do not communicate that He is the goal and the ground of joy in our suffering, then the very meaning of our suffering will be lost. The meaning is this: God is gain. God is gain. God is gain.[4]

JOHN PIPER
DESIRING GOD

EPILOGUE

Morning Joy

. . . weeping may remain for a night,
but rejoicing comes in the morning.

Psalm 30:5

AT TIMES I DO NOT FEEL WORTHY ENOUGH TO HAVE experienced this trial. God chose us to represent Christ to the world by the things we have suffered. He has given us several opportunities to share our story with others, both in small settings and in larger groups. Through those engagements, God showed us some of the good that had resulted from Hannah's death: changed lives, questions about God resolved, hearts turned back to Him, spiritual eyes opened. Was it worth losing our daughter so that others would know Christ deeper? Undoubtedly, yes. Was the price we paid worth seeing just one come to Christ for salvation? I can only answer this by asking another question: Did Christ consider the price He paid worth seeing me come to repentance? Knowing what my Savior sacrificed makes what I have given up for Him seem very small in comparison.

God has used our suffering to bring us closer to Him, and that is worth more to me than having Hannah back. I do not want to return to the way it was when she was alive. We have learned obedience to Christ more in our suffering than through our experiences in good times. I know for some this may be difficult to comprehend, and before this happened I would not have understood it myself. But the joy we felt as a result of standing firm and exalting Christ has made it all worth while.

This privilege of sacrificing for Christ was not always felt on a daily basis. God has worked healing into our lives little by little, with gentleness, patience, and love. Apart from His grace, there is no other explanation for the joy and gratitude we feel. After one full year of seeking God for peace, I am truly thankful for the gift of suffering. Losing our daughter hasn't been painless, but it has been good.

We have adjusted to life without Hannah, and I am at peace. I no longer believe that moving forward will betray her memory. We cry fewer times when thinking of her, visit her grave less often, and there have been nights when I have forgotten to sleep with her purple nightgown. Hannah will always be greatly missed and loved, but the expression of that love will have to wait until another season, one that will never end.

JOY UNEXPECTED
Phil Dufrin

To You my King I give my heart
And trust with all my being.
Though trial casts its shadow dark
And good no longer seeing.

I gave to You what seemed was mine
That which with care I tend.
Expecting it returned in time
No more in need of mend.

Yet when returned not as I thought
Your purpose dimmed by tears.
Great pain and grief to me You brought
Confronting dreaded fears.

The fear that I might not be whole
Without the ones I love.
You who sought and won my soul
Might fade from up above.

But with such mercy deep and pure
Your grace its shower fell.
Though faith besieged yet still secure
Love not to shrink but swell.

The skeptic's dart declares its doubt
That joy be found in grief.
They urge to let one's anger spout
And thus deny belief.

For whom shall I let anger flow
And rage for what was done.
My sovereign God has dealt this blow
That glory should be won.

Christ's glory did indeed prevail
In darkness joy shined through.
Your love removed grief's sullen veil
My heart to praise anew.

APPENDICES

Faith need never ask, "But what good did this do me?"
Faith already knows that everything that happens fits into
a pattern for good to those who love God. An
inconvenience is always, whether we see it or not, a
blessed inconvenience. We may rest in the promise that
God is fitting together a good many more things than are
any of our business. We need never see "what good it
did," or how a given trouble accomplishes anything. It is
peace to leave it all with Him, asking only that He do with
me anything He wants, anywhere, anytime, that God may
be glorified.[5]

ELIZABETH ELLIOT
A PATH THROUGH SUFFERING

I stood a mendicant of God before His royal throne
And begged Him for one priceless gift, which I could call my own.
I took the gift from out His hand, but as I would depart
I cried, "But Lord! This is a thorn, and it has pierced my heart!
This is a strange, a hurtful gift which Thou hast given me."
He said, "My child, I give good gifts and gave My best to thee."
I took it home, and though at first the cruel thorn hurt sore,
As long years passed I learned at last to love it more and more.
I learned He never gives a thorn without this added grace,
He takes the thorn to pin aside the veil which hides His face.[6]

MARTHA NICHOLSON

A Word About the Sovereignty of God in Suffering

Allow me to preface this section by stating that I am not an expert on this topic. A great many theologians have tackled the subject with far greater authority and persuasion. I have learned much about suffering and the sovereignty of God from reading books written by gifted authors such as Elisabeth Elliot and John Piper. Using their materials to help illuminate God's Word, I have formed a biblical view of God's sovereignty that may be difficult for many to accept but is nevertheless true.

Even at the risk of not doing it well, I would be remiss to not include a section of this book which addressed a biblical basis for God's sovereignty. As you read Hannah's story, our position on God's sovereignty as it relates to suffering should have been obvious: God is in control of all things, even those circumstances which cause us to suffer. He has planned and ordained them from before the foundation of the world.

Most Christians are familiar with the word "sovereign" and use it frequently to describe who God is. Webster's Dictionary defines it to mean, "above or superior to others; chief; greatest; supreme. One who exercises supreme power." I begin with this definition because what you think about God will affect how much control you think the Almighty has. Tell me your view of God, and I can almost always tell what you believe about His sovereignty. If you have a low, human-like view of God, then you might assume that only certain things are in His control. God is sovereign over all, but is at the mercy of man's will. Conversely, if you have a lofty, awesome view of a God who maintains supreme power, you would conclude that no event occurs outside of His knowledge. God is big enough to orchestrate all the details of human life, and no good or evil is outside His control. As you will read later, when looking at these two views in the light of Scripture, the latter is the correct position to have.

Assenting to the belief that God is in control of all things will undoubtedly spark many other questions. Why pray if God is going to do just as He planned anyway? Why does God hold man responsible for the choices he makes when those choices were ordained by Him? Does this mean that God is the author of sin and evil? How does salvation fit in with sovereignty? These are all questions that I have also grappled with, prayed for clarity about, and found answers to in the Scriptures. Since the scope of this chapter cannot possibly address each question, I can only exhort you to study it out for yourself. This is not a purposeful avoidance of these issues but a realization that these tough questions demand a personal search.

It is incorrect to think of God as interceding at certain times to change the direction of events to suit His will. Rather, He works in all things at all times to accomplish His perfect and holy will. Consider this example: You decide to leave work a little early to avoid bad weather. Once home, you receive word that there was a fatal multi-car accident on the freeway, and you missed it by minutes. In fact, if it hadn't been for getting off the exit and taking a different way home, you might have perished in the accident. You may think that God, who was taken off-guard by your decision to leave work early, caused you to vary your way home so that His purpose in allowing you to live another day would not be thwarted.

God's will does not change based on the actions and reactions of His people. Leaving work early on account of bad weather did not throw a wrench into God's plan, causing Him to respond to set it straight again. His design was that you would avoid the accident from the very beginning, and turning off the exit was the ordained means by which He carried this out. The phrase "in the wrong place at the wrong time" is a contradiction to the belief that

God is sovereign. According to God's plan, everything happens "in the right place and at the right time."

So how does this relate to suffering? Am I saying that God's will is for Christians to suffer? Yes—suffering is a *calling* of God. Trials of many sizes and kinds *will* come to all of us at one time or another, and, as 1 Peter 4:12 says, we are not to be surprised when they do: "*Do not be surprised at the painful trial you are suffering, as though something strange were happening to you.*"

Suffering is not an oddity in the Christian journey. The Bible is full of examples of men and women who have suffered for God's glory. Satan was given permission by God to inflict suffering upon Job's life. The disciples gave up everything to follow Jesus, and all but one of them died a martyr's death because they would not be quiet about the gospel. Take into account the life of Paul who, for Christ's sake, "lost all things," counting them as rubbish. These faithful saints understood God's call to suffer, and while they did not purposely look for trials or hope for painful hardships, they did choose to embrace the way in which God was working so that He may be glorified.

Surely you question how it could be God's will for His beloved people to suffer. The answers you seek can only come from the Word of God, the book of ultimate truth. In its pages you will find a wealth of passages relating to this topic. While studying the verses, you may wonder how they could have been so easily overlooked in the past. A few years before Hannah's death, the Lord led Phil and I on a similar search through the Bible. The truths we discovered became foundational to our faith, both in the good times and later, during our struggle through grief.

Read the following verses and ask God to soften your heart towards this truth. If you are already assured of God's sovereignty in suffering, these passages will help to reinforce your beliefs.

His wife said to him, "Are you still holding on to your integrity? Curse God and die!" He replied, "You are talking like a foolish woman. Shall we accept good from God, and not trouble?" In all this, Job did not sin in what he said. (Job 2:9-10)

To God belong wisdom and power; counsel and understanding are his. What he tears down cannot be rebuilt; the man he imprisons cannot be released. If he holds back the waters, there is no drought; if he lets them loose, they devastate the land. To him belong strength and victory; both deceived and deceiver are his. (Job 12:13-16)

When times are good, be happy; but when times are bad, consider: God has made the one as well as the other. (Ecclesiastes 7:14)

I form the light and create darkness, I bring prosperity and create disaster; I, the LORD, do all these things. (Isaiah 45:7)

I am God, and there is no other; I am God, and there is none like me. I make known the end from the beginning, from ancient times, what is still to come. I say: My purpose will stand, and I will do all that I please. From the east I summon a bird of prey; from a far-off land, a man to fulfill my purpose. What I have said, that I will bring about; what I have planned, that I will do. (Isaiah 46:9-11)

Who can speak and have it happen if the Lord has not decreed it? Is it not from the mouth of the Most High that both calamities and good things come? (Lamentations 3:37-38)

I know for some, especially those who have suffered sickness, loss, or death, this is a difficult truth to grasp. How could a loving God be so cruel? By trusting in God's sovereignty, Phil and I were spared from feeling angry and bitter towards Him. Our response to Hannah's death, though full of sorrow, was also one of great peace and joy. We trusted that there was a reason for having gone through this trial, one that we were content to let God reconcile in His own way and in His own time. Instead of asking God, "Why?" we asked, "How? How can we most glorify You through that which You have planned?"

God always has a purpose for our suffering, though we may not see it initially or even at all in this lifetime. He designs our trials as an integral part of a myriad of events that we know nothing about, and we must submit to His way of doing things. If you are wondering what might be God's intent for your personal suffering, the Scriptures are not silent when giving some of the reasons. For example, the verses in 1 Peter 1 and 4, tell us that the trials we experience are necessary for us, helping us to build trust in Christ, to prove our faith genuine, and to draw us closer to God.

You may have no desire to know God more deeply, especially if this means suffering might be the means which He uses to do this. But first consider: *What is your greatest good?* Is it the comforts that this short life offers? Is it having perfect emotional and physical health? King Solomon, the writer of Ecclesiastes, warns us that none of these things—pleasures, toil, riches, or advancement—will satisfy. After a life full of everything his heart desired, it all became meaningless. Our greatest good lies not in the things that the world needs to keep themselves "happy." On the contrary, *our greatest good is knowing God more and treasuring Him above all else.* Nothing else will bring us more joy and pleasure. And God's providence, both smiling and frowning, is the means by which we receive more of Himself.

Romans 8:28 is a verse that most Christians can recite from memory, but many struggle to reconcile it with a theology that does not view God as sovereign. *"And we know that in all things God works for the good of those who love him, who have been called according to his purpose."* Notice the words "all things." Did Paul mean only all *good* things?

The sovereignty we often ascribe to God is *our* definition of what God can or cannot do. As a result, we see Him as limited to purposing and accomplishing that which *we* define as good. From our perspective, there was nothing humanly good about Hannah's death and the grief that we experienced. But from God's viewpoint, this suffering was designed to bring us into a deeper place of obedience and surrender unto Him. And as I have attested in this book, there is nothing more satisfying or joyful than knowing our Savior more.

Our loving God is in complete control of our lives, both in times of pleasure and adversity. When the sun is shining down and the world is all is as it should be, direct your praise to Him for this comfortable life. Practice obedience to God during the good times so that you are ready to face the suffering when it comes. Press into Christ and learn how to hold loosely that which He gives. It will be less painful if He does not have to pry it out of your hand. There may be a time when God asks you to give up that which you treasure most. Will you be ready and willing?

Likewise, when the road is marked with suffering in whatever form, look to God and rejoice through the tears. You have been chosen by Him to bear on your body the marks of Jesus (Galatians 6:17) so that others will see Christ's love in you. How will you respond? The intensity of your pain will be determined more by your response to it than by the circumstances of your trial. Lean on Christ to pull you through, and trust in His promise to never leave you nor forsake you.

APPENDIX B

Help for Parents Whose Child Has Died

Having experienced the pain of losing a child, my heart burns with compassion for those who have gone through the same trial, both in the distant and recent past. I want to help ease their pain with the comfort that I have received. During the first year without Hannah I wish someone would have said, "I know how you feel." I longed for the companionship of another parent who had survived the pain with God's help and could "teach" me the "how-to" of grief. What I wanted but couldn't find was a grief mentor.

Following Hannah's death I regularly read the obituary section of the newspaper, searching for other families who had lost a child. I wanted to find someone with whom I could relate in my struggle through grief. When my search proved futile, I turned to the Christian bookstore for a book specifically about the death of a child, written by parents who had suffered through this loss. There wasn't much material on the subject to choose from. In part, that is why this book was birthed. My desire was not only to testify about God's faithfulness through our trial, but also to minister to other parents who are grieving the loss of a child, too. It is with this purpose that I write to you, suffering parent, from my own aching heart.

Along my journey through grief, there were several practical things I learned which helped me survive the pain of daily living. For those who have recently lost a child and are just beginning to walk the road towards restoration, much of what I learned will apply. For those parents who lost a child many years ago and are still struggling to move forward, take from my experience what you can, and look to God for the rest. We *do* have the loss of a child in common but each of our stories are different, and because of this, what helps us to heal will not be always be the same.

TURN FROM ANGER

I begin with this exhortation because the ability to heal hinges so much on this emotion. Your anger may be directed at the person whose neglectful behavior caused your child to die—a drunk driver, child care worker, or even your own spouse. Perhaps you are angry with the doctors and nurses who "didn't do enough" to save your child. Maybe you are angry with God—why didn't He answer your prayers and save your child from death? Anger that is not resolved will express itself in one way or another, and none of those forms are positive. When left uncontrolled, anger will only reap destruction to your family, your health, and to your relationship with God.

Phil and I never once felt anger towards God. The theology of God's sovereignty helped us to put Hannah's death in perspective and to see God work good through our trial. If your response to your child's death expressed anger towards God and you said, "It's not fair!", take heart, my friend. It's not too late to ask God to help you turn away from anger. He will help you, and He will forgive. Then, after you have found peace with God, ask Him to help you forgive those who may have contributed to your child's death.

Anger can be a paralyzing emotion that is only relieved by forgiveness. Decide who you are angry with, pray to God for His grace, and don't be controlled by bitterness. You will never be able to move forward and find peace unless you face it.

LOOK TO GOD FOR COMFORT

At times it may seem that you have been left all alone to deal with your grief. Very few can relate to the suffering that you have experienced. Yet there is One who knows exactly what you are going through—Jesus Christ. The Bible tells us that Christ, as our high priest, is able to sympathize with our weaknesses. On the cross, Christ suffered much physical and emotional pain as He was beaten for our transgressions and separated from the Father. Because of Christ's death, those who follow Him can *"approach the throne of grace with confidence, so that we may receive mercy and find grace to help us in our time of need"* (Hebrews 4:16). Do not hesitate to turn your grief over to God. He wants you to. And He *will* rescue you from despair, in His time and way.

Psalm 119:107 says, *"I have suffered much; preserve my life, O LORD, according to your word."* The promises of God, specifically those written to mourners, are accessible to you at any time. The Word is God's way of providing the comfort you need. *"My comfort in my suffering is this: Your promise preserves my life"* (Psalm 119:50). God will speak to your heart through the Scriptures, if you allow Him. The Psalms are a good place to begin, especially chapters 23, 77 and 119. It may even help to write out the most meaningful verses on index cards and display them where you can meditate on the words all throughout the day.

Memorizing the Scriptures will also enable you to call upon God's grace at any time and in any place. Soon after Hannah's death I decided to commit 1 Peter 1 to memory. It proved extremely valuable to me during those moments when it was hard to keep going.

Along with seeking God in the Scriptures, I also urge you to pray. "I've tried that and it still hurts," you may say. "God hasn't answered me, so why bother?" The writer of Psalm 77:1-2 felt the same way: *"I cried out to God for help; I cried out to God to hear me. When I was in distress, I sought the Lord; at night I stretched out untiring hands and my soul refused to be comforted."* It may seem as though your prayers are hitting the ceiling, and you wonder why God isn't responding. This isn't because He hasn't heard your cries for help. God promises to never leave nor forsake us. Confess to God what you feel. It doesn't have to be lengthy for God to understand; He already knows your heart. Or, if you have a hard time sorting through your feelings, write your prayers to God in a journal. Be assured that God "hears" the words you write as well.

STRENGTHEN YOUR MARRIAGE

The divorce rate among couples who have lost a child is high. The stress of dealing with life without your child takes its toll on the marital relationship. Don't let it. Make time to grieve with your spouse apart from your children. Spend a weekend away from home to read the Scriptures together, pray, and share memories.

Remember that each of you will grieve differently and usually not at the same time. It's best not to have any expectations as to how your spouse should be responding to your pain. Keep in mind that since both of you are grieving, it will be difficult to depend on one another for support.

There is a reason why God said, *"It is not good for the man to be alone. I will make a helper suitable for him"* (Genesis 2:18). This applies not only in the duties of everyday living but also during the wearisome seasons. You and your spouse need each other now more than ever as you work through your grief together. By concentrating on keeping your marriage intact, you may be surprised to find that your relationship grows to be the closest it has ever been.

SURRENDER THE NEED TO KNOW WHY

Asking God why your child has died is not a sin. Even Job, who lost literally everything, cried out to God for a reason. At first, God let Job "vent" without giving a response. He may do this in your life as well. Although it may take several months or even years to see it, God will show you the good that came from losing your child. In the meantime, don't try so hard to look for the reason. Lay this need aside or else it will control your life and steal away your joy.

Do not look at others and despise them for their prosperity, especially those who blatantly disregard God. You may be tempted to ask, "Why did this have to happen to our family? We have served God faithfully. Is losing our child the reward we get?" Even if you are solidly grounded in the belief that God is sovereign, these thoughts and questions are normal to have. While watching television at the hotel in Kalamazoo, Phil and I surfed the channels until a news program about Ozzy Osbourne caught our attention. We paused at the station long enough to hear how Mr. Osbourne had been in an accident while riding a four-wheeled recreational vehicle. His life was spared, and his family expressed their relief to the reporter. My response was to scowl at the program and ask Phil to turn the station. The thought came to mind, *God, why did You save this man's life and choose to take our daughter instead?* I had seen the "injustice" of our suffering and questioned God's plan. Quickly I repented of this attitude, resolving that I would be content to never fully understand God's plan for our loss.

If you are plagued with the need to know why God took your child away or are envious of others for having been spared suffering, I encourage you to turn to the Scriptures for reassurance of God's love and grace. And if God's silence is causing you to become angry with Him or is triggering depression, surrender the need to know the reason your child died. Continue to trust in His promise that *"in all things God works for the good of those who love him"* (Romans 8:28).

LET GO OF GUILT

Your child's death was no one's fault, not even yours. If you believe that God is sovereign over all events and circumstances, there is no reason to feel guilty. He has ordained the day of death for all people, your child included. Nothing you could have done would have thwarted His plan, for *"no one has power over the day of his death"* (Ecclesiastes 8:8).

Reading our story about Hannah may have caused you to compare your response with ours. Has guilt arisen because you feel that your response did not demonstrate strong faith? Looking back, you may be disappointed that opportunities were missed to use your suffering as a witness for Christ or that God was not glorified. I plead with you to not judge your faith by ours. Every parent's reaction to the death of their child is going to be different, and this, too, is ordained by God. Trust that God has used your response, whether "good" or "bad" to suit His purposes. We know that God had prepared us for Hannah's death years in advance. Only by His grace were we able to stand firm and not blame Him.

Unresolved guilt causes the wounds of grief to cut deeper. Search for what is causing you to feel guilty, and ask God to help you to forgive yourself or others. Perhaps you feel guilty for being angry with God. Confess this sin and He will forgive you. *"If we confess our sins, he is faithful and just and will forgive us our sins and purify us from all unrighteousness"* (1 John 1:9).

STUDY THE SCRIPTURES ABOUT HEAVEN

Aside from the Bible, one of the first books I read following Hannah's death was a book about heaven entitled *In Light of Eternity* by Randy Alcorn. In his book, Alcorn reviews the Scriptures and presents a biblical overview of where those who know Christ will spend eternity. Analyzing the Scriptures about heaven will help you to focus on where your child is instead of where he or she isn't. Most parents want the very best for their children. What could be better than walking on streets of gold and seeing Jesus face-to-face? The sadness that comes from missing Hannah is worth feeling when I consider her eternal happiness.

PERMIT YOURSELF TO CRY

Outwardly I am not an emotional person. I dealt with the pain of missing Hannah usually by crying privately, most often at night when alone with my thoughts. Although to others it may have appeared that I was not coping with my pain in a healthy manner, what they didn't see were the moments when I let it out while at home with my family.

Crying is a necessary part of grief. There is no shame in breaking down, either alone or in front of others. Feeling sad is not a sin and does not indicate that your faith is weak. Look at the example of Jesus and Lazarus in John 11. When Jesus finally came to Martha and Mary's house where Lazarus had died four days before, He saw the sisters weeping and was *"deeply moved in spirit and troubled."* When they took Jesus to see where Lazarus had been laid, Jesus cried because He loved Lazarus so much. If crying were the lone indicator of an individual's depth of faith, Jesus was one shallow person!

I found that spells of crying came over me without warning. I could not predict when they would begin, but I could allow myself to release the pain. Afterwards, I always felt better and was able to laugh again.

As time goes on, you will cry less often than in those first few weeks following your child's death. There were days when my eyes were continually wet. A year after Hannah's death I cried less often and for shorter periods. You may or may not experience a similar decrease in crying. One word of caution: be careful to guard against depression—make a *choice* against it every day.

DO NOT WITHDRAW FROM LIFE

Immediately after your child's death, you probably didn't feel like doing anything. Getting motivated to take care of yourself and your family was difficult because it forced you to face the "hole" left by your child. This is completely normal. Your world has been turned upside down and nothing will ever be the same again. It will take some time before the desire to ease into your routine returns.

This amount of time will vary from person to person—for me personally, it was almost one full year before all facets of life were in order again. At times I became stressed when all the pieces weren't together and had to remind myself that we were going through a big adjustment without Hannah. If this describes you, rest in the hope that God understands your struggle to move on with life. Don't feel guilty that things are being left undone. It won't be long before life resembles normalcy again, and you can always catch up later.

If it has been some time since your child has died and you are still struggling just to get out of bed in the morning, meditate on this verse: *"Because of the LORD's great love we are not consumed, for his compassions never fail. They are new every morning; great is your faithfulness"* (Lamentations 3:22-23). Take the first step and choose to receive His compassion which is poured out on you fresh every morning. This takes work, but you *can* do it. He will give you exactly what is needed to bear each day if you allow Him.

Remember that grief does cripple our ability to walk through life but should not paralyze us from moving forward. Start with tiny steps—a little progress is far better than withdrawing from life altogether. Given time, the burden of grief will lighten, and you will stride through the day as before.

HAVE NO EXPECTATIONS

This applies both to yourself and to others. Some experts have tried to categorize the experiences of grief as follows: shock, denial, tears, despair, confusion, depression, hope, and a new beginning. While all of these emotions are normal to feel, you may experience only some of them and not necessarily in that order. The important thing to remember is that each person grieves according to various stages and at different rates. Knowing this will help you to release others, such as a spouse or children, from any expectations you have for how they "should" be grieving.

When it comes to people outside your immediate family, don't be upset when they haven't said or done the "right" thing. Most people don't know what to say upon seeing you for the first time since the funeral. It will hurt when they fail to acknowledge your grief or to ask how your family is doing. Give them grace in this area. Before this happened, you may have responded the same way. And for those who do speak up but say the "wrong" thing, don't become offended. Talking about death makes some people uncomfortable, and in their nervousness they often say something inappropriate.

Lastly, do not assume that because people are silent, they aren't thinking about you and also missing your child. Most people would rather say nothing than to risk speaking something hurtful.

TALK OPENLY ABOUT YOUR CHILD

One way to help others know that you are comfortable talking about your child is to do the same yourself. Unless the listener feels very awkward discussing it, share the memories of your child as opportunities arise. That way others will feel more free to express their condolences because they know that talking about your child will not produce further pain.

I enjoy hearing from people how much they miss my daughter. It has been helpful to the healing process to know that she is still in their thoughts and memories. I hope that we never stop talking about Hannah.

KEEP THEIR MEMORY ALIVE

For some, this advice is obvious. They can't imagine putting away their child's photographs and mementos or not sharing the funny stories. But for others, the pain is so great that pictures come down off the walls and conversation is silenced as a way of coping. Avoiding the pain is not a healthy way to grieve. I believe it is easier to face the hurt and deal with it rather than keep your feelings inside where they will express themselves in other forms. Removing every article that reminds you of your child is a method of avoiding your emotions and will not aid the grieving process. Keep out the pictures, look at them often . . . and cry.

TAKE ADVANTAGE OF OTHERS

I don't mean this in a negative sense. It is wrong to use your grief to manipulate others into getting what you want. However, many will ask along the way if there is anything they can do to help. Don't allow your pride to keep you from answering yes! Initially, you won't have the energy to keep up with your normal duties; it will all be spent on grieving. Give others the opportunity to serve the Lord by serving your family. Be specific with your response by delegating chores that you need accomplished—meals, cleaning, laundry—and don't be embarrassed that your house isn't tidy when others come to lend a hand!

TALK TO YOUR OTHER CHILDREN

It's easy to become so focused on our own pain that we forget about the children who lost their sibling. We may think that our children are not affected by their brother or sister's death, especially if routine activities such as sleeping, eating, or playing, remain unchanged.

Like adults, children will react to death in different ways. Some will be more vocal about their feelings while others will say very little. Having both types of responses in our family, I learned how to be sensitive to each child's style. For the more quiet ones it is a good idea to frequently ask, "How are you feeling about your sister's death?" Most often you will only get a short answer: "I'm fine," or "It's OK." At least your child will know that it is acceptable to talk about their sibling in your presence.

Make sure that you bring up the happy times you shared together as a family while your child was alive. Refrain from discussing with your children only those things that evoke sad emotions. They should know that talking about their sibling will not always bring you distress.

At the same time, your children do not have to be reminded of their lost sibling every time a new memory is made. Phil and I caught ourselves doing this often: "Isn't this a fun day at the park? Hannah would have loved it . . . I wish she were here." Allow the happy times to be pure, untainted from the feelings of loss. Children sometimes need a break from always hearing about their departed sibling.

Be assured that while your children may not always show it, they do think about the sibling who has been taken from your family. If you are still unsure as to how they really feel, watch for changes in their behavior, and make a point to ask on a regular basis.

REALIZE THAT YOU WILL NEVER FULLY HEAL IN THIS LIFE

The irony of this wisdom is that by understanding you will never fully heal, you have just moved one step closer to restoration. You will find on your journey through grief that, while healing does come, you will never be whole again. A part of you died with your child. Don't expect the pain to cease to exist, even after the first anniversary of their death. Thoughts of your child will always cause a hesitation in your spirit as you reflect on what he or she meant to you.

An elderly friend of mine whose husband died several years before Hannah, once told me that although the pain will diminish over time, it doesn't ever go away completely. Instead of *healing*, you learn to *adjust* to life without the one you love. We will have to wait until the next life with Christ in order to be fully restored, both in body and spirit, and relationally as a family. Hold on to that hope when all else seems lost. Life is short, as we who have lost children can understand. It really won't be long until we are reunited with them again.

Our goal is not that our children be happy, fulfilled, and successful. Granted, we may desire these things for them. But our highest objective should be that our children would repent from their sins, put their trust in Jesus Christ, and reflect the gospel to the world around them.[7]

CAROLYN MAHANEY
FEMININE APPEAL

Childlike Faith
Reflections on Death From a Child's Perspective

While the death of our daughter was one of the most traumatic experiences of my life, I do know of something that would hurt me more severely—watching one of my children rebel against God. The hope we possessed throughout this trial came from the assurance that we will be reunited with Hannah again. Decades of separation are but specks of dust when compared to eternity.

I don't have to worry about Hannah anymore—she has made it to heaven and is safe with Jesus. But what about the spiritual condition of my other five children? Will they trust in Christ to redeem them from sin, or will they go their own way?

The salvation of my children's souls is the top priority of our parenting. In every aspect of life, Phil and I have pointed our children back to the cross of Christ, showing them their need for a Savior. We could provide our children with all of the material possessions, security, and love that might guarantee a "happy" life on this earth. But if the message of the gospel is not communicated day in and day out, none of those temporal pleasures will satisfy or bring them true joy. What really matters in the lives of our children is that they look to Christ for their salvation. He is the *only* way to heaven. He is the *only* way to find joy through all life's trials and tribulations. He is the *only* One who gives our lives purpose and meaning. Is there anything more important to want for our children than Christ alone?

Hannah's death has made a significant impact on her siblings, cousins, and friends. Not many of today's young people have experienced death so closely. The loss of Hannah has caused our children to reconsider their youthful invincibility. Thoughts about dying have produced doubt concerning the destiny of their own souls. They have pondered the brevity of life, realizing that death can arrive at anyone's doorstep, including that belonging to a four-year-old girl. These rather "adult" anxieties were forced upon our children at a young age, and, apart from Hannah's death, there may have been no other reason to consider them.

The year after Hannah passed away, I know of eight children, ages four to ten, who received Christ as their Lord and Savior: Vika, Moriah, Nathan, Natalie, C.J., Elliot, Hudson, and Benjamin. Two of these children belong to me! Both Moriah and Nathan responded to the gospel one morning in January after reading the Scriptures together. Recognizing their depraved, darkened hearts, they turned to Jesus and repented of their sins. Without a doubt, the death of their sister had been a major factor in this decision.

If losing our daughter was an event that God designed to bring children one step closer to Christ, then the pain we experienced was indeed worth it. Hannah's physical death has brought forth much spiritual life. This is one of the good things that God has allowed us to see as an outcome of our suffering. It has been a blessing to witness the little children come unto Him.

The children who knew and loved Hannah have a unique perspective on dying. They are not afraid of it, and some appear a little envious that she gets to live in heaven with Jesus. I asked some of these children to tell me what they have learned about life as a result of Hannah's death. I did not expect such mature responses. I pray that through these testimonies, God will increase your faith in the way that Jesus taught His disciples: *"I tell you the truth, unless you change and become like little children, you will never enter the kingdom of heaven"* (Matthew 18:3).

One of the things I learned when Hannah died was that life is very short. But someday I will see my sister again. I know that Hannah does not want to come back. I am sad that she is gone, but I am glad that she is in heaven with Jesus, maybe even sitting on His lap.

One of the things I miss doing with Hannah is playing her favorite game with her, which was called Scoops. One of the things I remember doing with Hannah was going out to the chicken coop before the chickens had started laying eggs. When we entered the coop, we discovered the first egg. I ran back to the house with Hannah yelling, "Wait!" in her little voice. That voice is something I will always remember.

--Moriah, age 9

When Hannah died I felt sad, but we were happy that she could be with God. We are not going to live on earth forever. When we die we go to heaven if we believe that we are sinners.

Hannah was my sister Emma's best friend. I liked her because she was nice.

--Elliot, age 8

I love Hannah, and I really miss her a lot. I wish I could see her again, and I will someday in heaven. When our families got together we would play a lot. Hannah always played nicely.

When my mom and dad told me that Hannah died, I didn't believe them. I thought Daddy was kidding. When I knew she had died I was really sad, and I cried.

In heaven, Hannah is having a good time. That makes me feel happy.

--Brennan, age 6

Hannah was nice and very kind and gentle. She liked to play with me a lot. She was generous, and she was my best friend when she died. When she died I was very sad. I was thinking that was the thing that God wanted Hannah to do. I will never see her again in this land, but I'll see her in heaven someday.

I learned that Hannah will have more fun up there than down here. She had a chance to go home. And if she had a choice, she would choose heaven because that's a better place for her.

--Emma, age 5

I was really stunned when my parents told me, but I am glad that she died because now she gets to worship Jesus every day. What a privilege that is! I know that God ordained her death, and some of my aunts and uncles heard the Word of God [at her funeral].

My favorite thing about Hannah was playing Uno with her.

--Nathan, age 7

When Hannah died I was sad, but at the same time I was joyful because I knew she was having the best time in heaven. I knew she was with Jesus, and she was happy.

I learned that God is always in control, and that although we don't know why something happens, there is always a reason. We need to trust God because He is working somehow through all situations.

My memories of Hannah: She was always smiling; she was "Hannah Banana"; she was always so happy.

--Tory, age 12

I liked Hannah because she was my friend. I was sad that she died. I'm glad she's in heaven. Hannah is having fun there. Maybe she is talking to God. Even though we are sad that Hannah died, it was for a good reason because she's in heaven now. You can't get sick or hurt in heaven. When we believe in Christ, we go to heaven and be with God.

--Hudson, age 6

When my mom and dad told us that Hannah died, I remember sitting on the couch and crying. My stomach hurt because I was so sad. It was hard to think that I would never see her again on earth. I miss her cute little way of saying "no." But what I miss most of all about Hannah is her character. She was always so bright, full of life, and she loved to do stuff.

I know it is better for Hannah to be up in heaven with Jesus, but I think of her often, and I miss her a lot. I will someday see her again in heaven.

--Ian, age 10

When my mom and dad told me that Hannah died, at first I thought they were joking, but then I realized that they were serious. Then I remember going up to my room, crying. My stomach hurt so bad because I was trying to fight back the tears. The worst thing of all was thinking that I would never see her on earth again.

I miss her little "yes" and "no" the most of all. I know that Hannah is so happy in heaven and that it is better for her. And I also know that I will see her someday in heaven with Jesus.

--Colette, age 9

When Hannah died I felt like there was a hole in our family. It started me thinking about being a servant of Christ.

The good thing about it [her death] is that she won't have any more problems with her health. Now she is perfect in heaven.

I will always remember her! I remember that Hannah was always nice, and she would make me laugh. She loved to color and draw, too.

--C.J., age 9

I was sad when Hannah died. I was praying for her when she was in the hospital. After she died I thought a lot about Hannah's family and how they knew that God was with them, and that made me feel happy!

I really liked to play with Hannah. I will always love her. I remember that Hannah had really pretty hair and a pretty face.

--Maddie, age 7

When Hannah died I was really sad. God showed me what Jesus dying on the cross really meant. I knew that Hannah was in heaven with Jesus Christ. I was sad for my family but happy for Hannah.

I remember running around and playing with Hannah at church. I love her and will always miss her!

--Doug, age 10

When I think about Hannah, I think about her family on that Sunday when my mom and dad told us kids that Hannah had gone to be with Jesus. I thought about Moriah and her siblings, and I said to myself, "What is this going to do to the Dufrin family as well as to those who knew her?"

Moriah, Nathan, Abigail, and Samuel, along with Mr. and Mrs. Dufrin, all came to church that Sunday, and we all felt we did not know what to say. When we got home, I went to my bedroom and cried. I just missed Hannah so much. I was so sad when Hannah passed away. But now I know that she is happy and she has no more problems.

What about Hannah do I miss? EVERYTHING! The way she pushed her glasses on to her nose (they were always falling off); the way she loved you; and everything else. When I hear the song "Homesick" by Mercy Me, I want to be with Hannah. When they sing the phrase, "I close my eyes, and I see your face. If home is where your heart is then I'm out of place," I want to close my eyes and open them and see Hannah running around pushing up her glasses.

It has been such a great witness to those around the Dufrin family, to unbelievers and believers. Many people have come to love Hannah even after she died. It was all part of God's big perfect plan. Instead of crying, we should rejoice for God's plan is never wrong.

Hannah can now dance ballet with Jesus by her side in heaven's flowers.

--Emily, age 10

APPENDIX D

Resources for Grieving Parents

Alcorn, Randy. *In Light of Eternity.* Colorado Springs: WaterBrook, 1999. This was the first book I read after Hannah's death; it was just what I needed to realign my perspective. Alcorn does an excellent job presenting an overview of what the Bible says about heaven and how this should affect the way we live on earth.

Bruce III, James W. *From Grief to Glory.* Wheaton, Ill.: Crossway Books, 2002. A story of one family's walk through the grief of losing their infant son, and how the writings of Luther, Calvin, Bach, Spurgeon and many others, helped them to find comfort.

Elliot, Elizabeth. *A Path Through Suffering.* Ann Arbor, Mich.: Servant Publications, 1990. This was one of the most life-impacting books that I have ever read. Elliot asks the difficult questions about why God allows us to suffer and provides answers from the Word.

MacArthur, John. *Safe in the Arms of God.* Nashville: Thomas Nelson, 2003. An analysis of the Scriptures concerning the eternal destination of a child's soul. An encouraging read, especially if you have lost an infant through miscarriage or stillbirth.

Piper, John. *Desiring God.* Sisters, Oreg.: Multnomah, 1986. I find Piper's works to be challenging, both in wording and content. But no other book has helped to shape my theology more. In his book, Piper reveals that God is most glorified when we are most satisfied in Him. He calls this "Christian Hedonism." The 1996 version includes a chapter on suffering for God's glory and how to find joy through the pain.

Piper, John. *The Hidden Smile of God.* Wheaton, Ill.: Crossway Books, 2001. Phil read this book shortly after Hannah died. Piper draws from the biographies of three faithful men of the past—John Bunyan, William Cowper, and David Brainerd— to demonstrate how honoring God in the midst of affliction will bear much fruit.

Rankin, Peg. *Yet Will I Trust Him.* Ventura, Calif.: Regal Books, 1980. If you are struggling to understand the biblical meaning of sovereignty, Rankin's book will address all your questions in an easy-to-read format. I haven't been able to find a more recent publication on this topic that parallels her thorough work of analyzing the Scriptures.

Wiersbe, David W. *Gone but Not Lost.* Grand Rapids: Baker Books, 1992. This is a scripturally sound self-help book about what to expect when grieving the death of a child. It offers practical help to parents as they cope with grief, marriage, family, and life in general. The promises of God and reliance on Him for strength are the principal tenets of Wiersbe's valuable counsel.

NOTES

1. David Livingstone, quoted in John Piper, *Desiring God* (Sisters, Oreg.: Multnomah, 1986), p. 204.

2. Charles Swindoll, "Taking on Life with a Great Attitude," *Insights Newsletter*, June 2005 (Plano, Tex.: Insight for Living).

3. John Piper, *Desiring God* (Sisters, Ore.: Multnomah, 1986), p. 235.

4. Ibid., p. 238.

5. Elisabeth Elliot, *A Path Through Suffering* (Ann Arbor, Mich.: Servant Publications, 1990), pp. 59-60.

6. Martha Nicholson, quoted by John Piper in a sermon, "To Be a Mother is a Call to Suffer", http://www.desiringgod.org/library/ sermons/ 01/051301.html

7. Carolyn Mahaney, *Feminine Appeal* (Wheaton, Ill.: Crossway Books, 2004), pp. 60-61.

The author would appreciate hearing how God has used this book to help you. Please send your comments and testimonies to:

Sandy Dufrin
P.O. Box 144
Williamston, MI 48895

You may also e-mail her at: psdufrin@acd.net

26775717R00155

Made in the USA
Middletown, DE
05 December 2015